A CATHOLIC LOOKS AT BILLY GRAHAM

A Catholic Looks at Billy Graham

by

Charles W. Dullea, S.J.

PAULIST PRESS
New York / Paramus / Toronto

Library of Congress
Catalog Card Number: 73-88904

ISBN 0-8091-1804-1

Cover design by Rus Anderson

Published by Paulist Press
Editorial Office: 1865 Broadway, N.Y., N.Y. 10023
Business Office: 400 Sette Drive, Paramus, N.J. 07652

Printed and bound in the
United States of America

ACKNOWLEDGMENTS

Grateful acknowledgment is made to Dr. Robert O. Ferm of
The Billy Graham Evangelistic Association who read this book in
manuscript form and made many valuable suggestions.

Acknowledgment is also made to several sources for permission
to quote from the writings of Billy Graham: to *Decision* magazine
for excerpts from two articles, ©1964 and 1968 by The Billy Graham
Evangelistic Association, and from *Facts, Faith and Feeling* by
Billy Graham, ©1957 by The Billy Graham Evangelistic Association;
to Doubleday & Company, Inc., for permission to reprint from *The
Challenge* by Billy Graham, © 1969 by Billy Graham and from
Peace With God by Billy Graham, © 1953 by Billy Graham; to the
Reader's Digest for permission to reprint an excerpt from the May,
1969 article "What the Bible Says to Me" by Billy Graham; to
The Ecumenical Review (Geneva, Switzerland: World Council of
Churches) for permission to quote from "Conversion, a Personal

Revolution" by Billy Graham, Vol. XIX, No. 3, July 1967; to *The Christian Century* for permission to quote from the February 17, 1960 article "What Ten Years Have Taught Me" by Billy Graham,© 1960 by The Christian Century Foundation.

Finally, acknowledgment is made to E. P. Dutton & Co., Inc., for permission to use a quote of Paul Tillich from *Faith Is a Star*, written and edited by Roland Gammon, © 1963 by the Southern Baptist Convention Radio and Television Commission; to Fleming H. Revell Company for permission to quote from *The Psychology of Christian Conversion* by Robert O. Ferm, © 1959 by Fleming H. Revell Company; to Alba House for permission to quote from *Theology of Revelation* by Rene Latourelle, S.J.; to Seabury Press for permission to quote from *Sacramentum Mundi,* Vol. 2, edited by Karl Rahner,©1968 by Herder KG; and to Harcourt Brace Jovanovich for permission to quote from "The Hollow Men" by T. S. Eliot, from *Collected Poems 1909-1962.*

CONTENTS

For

Winnie and Charlie

Preface

This book is an adaptation of a doctoral dissertation written for the Gregorian University in Rome on Billy Graham's theology of conversion. It is based first of all on Graham's own writings: 12 books (excluding reprints under titles other than the original), about 165 published radio sermons, his articles in *Decision* magazine (one a month since its inception in 1960), numerous published interviews, statements, articles, speeches. It also made use of the extensive material on Graham, about 70 books, as well as innumerable articles, ranging from serious studies in scholarly journals to popular treatments in the mass media.

As background for this book I attended crusades in Shea Stadium, New York in the summer of 1970 and in Oakland, California in the summer of 1972; on both occasions I met and talked with Mr. Graham. There was also a rather lengthy telephone conversation with him on religion and politics.

I visited the headquarters of the Billy Graham Evangelistic Association in Minneapolis three times, to work in the excellent research library there and meet and talk with various members of the Graham organization. There were two conferences with Dr. Robert Ferm, Graham's director of research, in Minneapolis and Atlanta, and one meeting with Dr. Walter H. Smyth, vice-president in charge of crusades. Further familiarity with crusade procedures and organization was gained from a visit to the "follow-up room" at Shea Stadium during the June 1970 crusade, while some hundred volunteers were processing "decision cards."

The whole Graham organization, from Billy Graham on down, were most helpful. They weren't quite sure just what I was up to, or what would emerge eventually, possibly to haunt them, but gave their courteous cooperation just the same, willingly and courageously.

C. W. D.

1. The Man Who Won't Go Away

For the student of religion in twentieth-century America, William (Billy) Franklin Graham is a phenomenon that cannot be ignored. No evangelist in history has been heard by more people. A preacher of rare power, he has in the past 25 years preached the gospel to immense crowds, not only in his native United States but in Europe, Africa, India, Latin America, the Far East and Australia. He preaches anywhere there is space for a big crowd—auditoriums, theaters, concert halls, football stadiums, public parks—to multitudes which number sometimes in the scores of thousands.

In Kottyam, India, 100,000 people sat on the hillsides to listen, more than half of them having walked ten to twenty miles to hear him. In Los Angeles, in the Memorial Coliseum in 1963, the crowd numbered 134,254. In Berlin, at Brandenburg Gate, in 1960 before The Wall was thrown up, nearly 100,000 people from both East and West Germany gathered in the "Plaza of the Republic" for the closing meeting of the Berlin crusade.

Reinhold Niebuhr, certainly no unqualified admirer, said of him, "This handsome, youthful, modest and obviously sincere evangelist is better than any evangelist of his kind in American history".

An estimated 60 million people have heard Graham in person in nearly every state of the USA and in some 60 foreign countries. But this is only his face-to-

3

face audience. The modern miracle of television has multiplied Graham's presence many, many times. First, there is the closed-circuit TV hookup which brings Graham's crusades "live" to places too numerous for him to visit personally. Thus in Britain in 1967, 25 cities were linked for ten days to carry his message from Earl's Court, London, into every part of England and southern and central Scotland. The screens were large, 30 feet high and 40 feet wide, and it is said that the impact of his preaching was as great as if Graham were present in person.

In April 1970 the Westfalenhalle in Dortmund, West Germany was packed, with television beaming the crusade to 35 European cities in 11 countries, including Yugoslavia. It is difficult to say how many heard Graham on this occasion, but the crusade headquarters reported 15,000 "decisions for Christ".

In recent years large crusades are often filmed for television, then later shown to audiences of millions across the United States on national or regional telecasts, and in other countries as well. John Pollock, a keen student of the Graham phenomenon, says: "Television crusades form Billy Graham's most extensive and effective ministry in North America, in black and white at first, in color since the 1966 London crusade". His televised crusades are regularly bought by some 235 local TV stations. With three or more series a year, each comprising several one-hour telecasts, he reaches nearly every home in the United States, and is watched and listened to by men and women in all walks of life, Catholics and Jews as well as Protestants, by many who would never go near a church. After a national telecast, the Graham headquarters in Minneapolis receives anywhere from 500,000 to one million letters.

Radio is another outlet for the Graham message. His sermons are heard on more than a thousand stations by 20 million people in the United States, and on 30 short-wave stations around the world on a program called "The Hour of Decision", which has been broadcast since 1950.

Nor does he neglect the printed word. Not content with writing books, one of which, *Peace With God*, sold over two million copies in 38 languages, in 1960 he founded a monthly magazine called *Decision*. This is a popular periodical, with "something for everybody", the confirmed Christian as well as the unchurched, youth as well as the mature. The typical issue contains a sermon or article by Billy Graham, a Bible lesson, an inspirational "testimony" from someone who has found Christ, news of the crusades and other activities of the Graham organization. It is an attractive bit of journalism, professionally done, well written, well edited, handsomely illustrated with color photos. In a short ten years it has climbed to a circulation of four million, the largest circulation of any religious periodical in the world. There are special editions for Britain and Australia, and French and German editions as well. There is also a Japanese edition, part in Japanese and part in English, and a Spanish edition for Latin America, prepared in Buenos Aires and printed in Minneapolis. Out of the magazine *Decision* has grown a subsidiary apostolate, a Summer School of Christian Writing, to improve the quality of religious writing, with a couple of hundred in attendance every year from many countries.

In 1952 the Graham Association made its first religious film, *Mr. Texas*, on a budget of $30,000. That film is still circulating, but has been joined by many others. The showing of these films is organized like a crusade, with teams of counsellors trained in advance, and an invitation to the audience for a decision or commitment to Christ. *The Restless Ones* was released in 1965 and in two years was shown in 852 cities, with a total attendance of almost three million, and almost 200,000 "inquirers", who responded to the invitation to come forward and make a "decision for Christ". From the Paris office a team of nine full-time "film evangelists" supervises the European distribution of these films, some in English, some dubbed into European languages. It is estimated that every 35 minutes a Billy Graham film is shown somewhere around the world.

Everything Graham does seems to be big. He has a syndicated column called *My Answer* with spiritual advice for inquirers, which appears in 146 newspapers with a circulation of 22 million. At the World's Fair in New York in 1964-65, the most prominent part of the skyline was the 117 foot high tower of the Billy Graham Pavilion. More than five million people visited the pavilion, and more than one million people from 125 countries viewed the religious film *Man in the Fifth Dimension*, during which Graham gave the invitation to accept Christ. Thousands of inquirers responded to this invitation and came forward to be counselled.

The size of these efforts of evangelism sometimes boggles the imagination. When Graham came to Los Angeles in 1963, he came at the invitation of the Southern California Council of Churches. More than 3,500 individual congregations were involved in an entire year of preparation. Some 23,000 people applied for the counseling classes, about 15,000 completed the course, and 7,000 finally were accepted as counsellors and advisors. Each night of the crusade the choir numbered between 3,000 and 5,000; 20,000 church members called in advance on 1,000,000 homes to invite attendance at the crusade. And as opening day drew near, 80,000 women met for 15-minute prayer meetings in 10,000 homes, led by Cliff Barrows, Graham's song leader and master of ceremonies, in specially recorded radio programs.

The Association's main office in Minneapolis, with 400 salaried workers plus many volunteers, mails out the four million copies of *Decision* every month, processes the 100,000 changes of address after each of these mailings, opens, sorts and answers well over two million letters every year. After a typical crusade, that of Australia in 1969 for instance, 100 people did nothing but sort incoming mail into various categories. To keep up with the avalanche they worked two 10-hour shifts daily, including Saturdays.

Graham multiplies even more these far-flung operations by the use of "associate evangelists". These are a team of ten men who, when not helping Graham with one of his crusades, are off somewhere else conducting "associate crusades". They are all excellent evangelists in their own right, handpicked by Graham himself, using the Graham resources, organization, general methods, and preaching the Graham gospel. Perhaps the most effective is Leighton Ford, a Canadian and Billy's brother-in-law, who has his own team of organizers and assistants, just like Graham has for his crusades. These associate crusades are preached not only in the United States but in India, Africa, Asia, Latin America and all over the world. Their number has steadily increased. Without counting the overseas crusades, 30 were held in 1970 and almost 50 in 1971.

Graham in one sense is more than a single man. He is an institution, an organization, a trademark. He is a symbol, further, of a world-wide thrust of a particular brand of Christianity, the biblical, evangelical kind, intent on preaching the Gospel to every creature.

But he is more than just a symbol of this evangelical thrust. He is the effective focus, rallying point and spearhead of the movement called evangelical. He makes a determined effort to strengthen and deepen the evangelical movement throughout the world. Thus, several years ago he made a practice of meeting on a regular basis with a small group to discuss the possibility of a world congress on evangelism in which leading evangelicals from every part of the world could come together, face the issues which confront them, and state again the theological basis of evangelism. These meetings eventually resulted in the World Congress of Evangelism in Berlin, October 25 to November 4, 1966. The magazine, *Christianity Today*, whose executive editor, Dr. L. Nelson Bell, is Graham's father-in-law, sponsored the Congress, and the Graham Association supplied the organizational know-how, planned it for three years, paid for the transportation of some of the poorer delegates. Graham, as honorary chairman, gave the keynote and final addresses, chaired the evening sessions, and was the guiding hand of the Congress. In Berlin he clearly assumed the role of world leader of the evangelical movement.

To his fellow Americans, he is certainly the best known clergyman in the country. Friend of four Presidents, for the last 20 years he has had easy access to the White House, although, as he points out, he has never visited without an invitation. President Eisenhower asked him to prepare the religious aspects of his inauguration, and in 1957, just before deciding to send federal troops into racially tense Little Rock, Arkansas, to integrate the schools, he phoned Graham from the White House. Billy visited the White House when Kennedy was President, and he was a frequent caller on President Johnson. He offered the prayer at the Nixon inaugural, and was the first cleric to preside at the special White House Sunday morning services that Mr. Nixon inaugurated. In fact, President Nixon attended the crusade at Knoxville, Tennessee, in May 1970 and spoke there, the first time a President of the United States had ever addressed a revival meeting.

On the Fourth of July, 1970, at special Independence Day religious-patriotic ceremonies Graham spoke to the whole country from the steps of the Lincoln Memorial via national television, calling upon his audience of millions to return to or deepen their faith in God and their American heritage. Millions of Americans annually put him high on their hero list, as is shown by the fact that every year since 1951 he has been named to the select Ten Most Admired Men in the World, in the annual survey conducted by the Gallup Poll.

He is almost as well known abroad as at home. In his crusades the percentage of "decisions for Christ" is much higher in Germany than in the United States. He went to Tokyo in July 1970, to address the convention of representatives of the 31 million strong Baptist World Alliance. "Abroad", as *Newsweek* says, "Graham is definitely Mr. American Protestant, and perhaps even Dr. Christian". According to James Kilgore, "He probably is the best known Christian in the world, with the possible exception of the pope; assuredly he is the most widely known preacher".

As might be expected, a person so prominent is bound to be criticized. He has been judged by different people in wildly different ways. For example:

Billy Graham is more than a preacher, more than an evangelist, more than a Christian leader. In a greater sense, he has become our conscience.
(Then Governor) John Connally of Texas

Billy Graham is a false teacher who is doing more harm to the cause of Christ than any living man.
Dr. Bob Jones, Jr.

I only wish we had half a dozen men of his caliber to go forth and do likewise.
Cardinal Cushing of Boston

If he persists in making common cause with those who deny the Word of God . . . the verdict of church history will be that (he) will be known as the greatest divider of the Church of Christ in the twentieth century.
Dr. Charles J. Woodbridge

Reinhold Niebuhr attacked Graham's biblical literalism and what Niebuhr considered his oversimplification of the Christian religion without enough regard to the social implications and applications of the Gospel. Niebuhr deprecated his "pietistic fundamentalism" and its great emphasis on "decision for Christ" as the basis for the solution to all of life's problems.

In the New York crusade of 1957, when the Protestant churches of the city faced the issue of whether or not they should endorse Graham's evangelistic effort, minorities at both ends of the theological spectrum fought endorsement tooth and nail. The liberals predicted that much harm would be done to the churches by what they regarded as his simplistic reactionary theology. The militant fundamentalists declared that Billy had gone over to the modernists.

Still others criticize his methods of "engineering mass consent" in his crusades, claiming that he is inducing a superficial "decision for Christ" by psychological tricks. Some, like Malcolm Boyd and G.W. Target, base their disapproval on grounds of the freedom and dignity of the human person. Others, such as Erroll Hulse, base their disagreement on theological grounds, contending that in the Graham theology there is too much emphasis on decision and the free will of man, not enough on the sovereign will of God, thus contradicting one of the basic principles of historic Protestant theology.

McLoughlin, toward the conclusion of his *Modern Revivalism*, predicted, not in explicit terms but implicitly and equivalently, the imminent decline of Billy Graham by comparing his career to that of other popular American evangelists who faded from the scene after a brief heyday: "Finney, Moody, Sam Jones and Billy Sunday had maintained their popularity for only about ten years. Graham's decline might be gradual, as were those of Finney, Jones and Moody, or it might be precipitous, like that of Sunday".

McLoughlin's book was published in 1959. In the intervening years, Graham's work, far from declining, has grown immensely. In *Decision* magazine for January 1973, Dr. Walter Smyth, director of crusades, reports that Graham had received 8,400 requests to speak in the last year. Just the 1973 crusade schedule, besides Atlanta, Minneapolis-St. Paul, Raleigh, St. Louis and several smaller American cities, includes, with the help of "associate evangelists", a six-week crusade in six major cities of Korea, as well as other crusades in Durban, South Africa, Jamaica and Guam.

Here is a recent confirmation of the continuing Graham appeal. The *International Herald-Tribune* for June 1, 1973, p. 16, reports: "Evangelist Billy Graham has outdone himself. The opening night of his five-day crusade in Seoul, South Korea, drew a throng of 516,000 —his largest in 33 years of barnstorming for God. The previous record was 200,000, set at a 1960 rally in Rio de Janiero".

"Graham's hour-long sermon received running translation by a Korean pastor, against the background of a 6,000 voice choir. After the sermon, 20,000 Koreans responded to his call for 'decisions for Christ'. About 3,000 remained for overnight prayers".

Anyone studying the religious scene had better look at Billy Graham. He is very much with us. He is the man who won't go away.

2. Early Years and Theological Stance

Early Years: Charlotte to Los Angeles

To understand a person's mature thought and life style it helps to know his family background and early life. An appreciation of St. Paul's earlier career as a Pharisee of the Pharisees helps us to realize how shocking must have been the revelation of the "mystery", that all men, even Jews, were to be saved not by the works of the Mosaic law but by faith in Jesus Christ, and how vividly therefore this must have been impressed on his consciousness. Similarly, an understanding of Luther's tormented sense of sin as an Augustinian monk helps us grasp better his later exhilarating sense of freedom in a caution-to-the-winds type of trust in the merits of Christ.

But early antecedents do not always result in a contrary reaction. With Billy Graham, it is not reaction but continuity that we see. Today's evangelist, uncompromising preacher of faith in Jesus Christ, apostle of the Bible as the inerrant word of God, upholder of the Protestant ethic of thrift and hard work, advocate of the old-fashioned virtues of rural America, came from just that kind of background. His early life did nothing but implant and nurture that sort of development. There is no turn-about in the career of Billy Graham, no break with continuity, no uprooting from the early planting.

He comes from tough, durable Scotch-Irish stock,

all four of his grandparents being descended from the pioneers who settled in the Carolinas before the American Revolution. Billy, or more formally, William Franklin Graham, Jr., was born on a farm on the outskirts of Charlotte, North Carolina, on Nov. 7, 1918, the eldest child of William Franklin Graham and Morrow Coffey Graham. There were three other children, a boy and two girls, the youngest fourteen years younger than Billy Frank, as he was called in those days.

The farm, left by Billy's grandfather to his father and uncle, consisted of 300 acres, enough to maintain a fair-sized herd of dairy cows. The family was moderately well off, not rich, but by no means poor either. They had hired men, a colored foreman whom young Billy greatly admired, a colored maid. They owned a car, and later a new brick house with indoor plumbing, a sign of modernity and middling affluence for that time and place. The dairy business with its four hundred customers afforded a comfortable living to the six Grahams. But they had to work hard for this moderate comfort. Billy Frank was up every morning long before dawn to help milk the 75 cows, and then deliver the milk by truck. After school it was more work, milking again and whatever else had to be done around the farm. Mr. Graham was uncomfortably conscious of the many agricultural bankruptcies in that period in the Carolinas, and during the depression he lost all his savings in a series of bank failures. He had to deny himself and his family many luxuries. It was, all in all, not poverty but a simple life without frills.

The Grahams belonged to the Associate Reformed Presbyterian Church, and faithfully made the five-mile drive every Sunday to the austere services conducted in the Reformed Presbyterian style which forbade any songs except psalms. The moral code of the Grahams was strict: no swearing, smoking, drinking, dancing, gambling. A story is told that Billy's father, when Prohibition was repealed in 1933, made him and his sister Catherine drink a whole bottle of beer, which made him forever after dislike the taste of liquor and eradicated any desire he might have had for it.

Billy's parents were seriously religious, especially Mrs. Graham after 1933 when she joined a Bible class, where personal piety was emphasized. Frank Graham had been converted in his youth. This conversion deserves some attention. He tells the story himself:

I was eighteen years old I guess, when three old Confederate soldiers . . . were holding a meeting in the Dillworth Methodist church. . . . One Sunday evening —I had been to a dance on Saturday night and I felt pretty bad on Sunday morning—I went to the meeting and when I went in I felt like I would die before I sat down. I was under conviction from the time I hit the door. Well, when the preacher dismissed the congregation I sat on. They came back to me and wanted to know if they could help me. I said "I don't know what is wrong with me, I'm in bad shape". They said, "Come up and let us pray with you". They did, but I went on for about ten days and nights unable to eat or sleep. I cared nothing for this world nor anything the world had to offer. I wanted something that the world couldn't give and I believed that I would know it when I got it. That was what I was looking for. Well, I prayed, I read the Scripture, and they were having prayer meetings for me until I gave up as a hopeless case. Satan said: "You have gone too far, you have committed the unpardonable sin". I didn't know it was Satan talking to me, but I do now.

One night just as I turned off Park Road, the road I live on, into Worthington Avenue, God saved me and my eyes were opened, and old things passed away and all things became new. I will never forget that moonlit night. When I went into the church I was shaking hands with folks with a different face, and the first man whose hand I shook was saved without my speaking to him. He never forgot it, because he saw the Spirit in my face and he knew that there had been a change. I went to his funeral years later. He stayed saved.

It would seem that this religious fervor cooled somewhat in later life. But he always lived a good Christian life, and was known for his honesty. However, the farm must have absorbed all his interest and attention, so much so that Billy Graham is quoted as saying: "They went to church, but beyond that they never talked religion. They never acted religious". But after an accident that Frank suffered while sawing wood and a full recovery that seemed an answer to prayer, both he and his wife believed that the Lord really "spoke to them" and "that they should find more time for Bible study and prayer".

Billy Frank wasn't much of a student, being too full of nervous energy and too interested in other things to concentrate on books; nor were the teachers of the best. However young Graham loved history and read a hundred books on this subject including Gibbon as well as Charles and Mary Beard.

At the time of his conversion at the age of 16, he was in a sense not a very apt subject. That is, he was not what would normally be regarded as a great sinner. He was fond of girls, and they of him, but in an innocent, wholesome way. He was too busy for dalliance. He was rowdy and mischievous, played boyish pranks, was a little wild, racing the family car at high speed around the countryside. One night he travelled over 200 miles in such races. He himself says he was "rebellious". By this he probably means he felt the Lord wanted him to settle down and get serious with his life, and Billy was fighting that kind of dedication. He wasn't ready for it.

In 1934 Mordecai Ham, the evangelist, came to Charlotte to conduct a revival. Ham by all accounts was an eloquent speaker with a "tendency to frighten men into heaven by dangling them over hell". Billy, urged by his friend Albert McMackin, went to the revival. McMackin says: "I figured he was the same way that I had been, a moral boy with a head knowledge taught by his own people, but not having come face to face with the Lord Jesus Christ".

Graham tells the story in his own words:

I don't recall what Mordecai Ham preached about that night, but I remember that I sat spellbound . . . The fascination of an old-fashioned revival is hard to explain to anybody who never experienced one. The crowd seems to be gripped by a unity of consecration, but was much more intense than during regular services. Each listener became deeply involved with the evangelist who had an almost embarrassing way of describing your sins and shortcomings and demanding on pain of divine judgment that you mend your ways. As I listened, I began to have thoughts I had never known before. Something began to speak to my heart.

However, he didn't go forward, but came back to the meeting, fascinated, night after night. He tried to get away from the gaze of the preacher by hiding behind a lady with a big hat, and then he joined the choir to be out of his line of vision, even though he couldn't sing very well. But Ham preached, "He that being often reproved and hardeneth his neck shall suddenly be cut off". . . . Several hundred worshippers gathered before the pulpit when the choir switched to "Almost persuaded Christ to believe". Billy Frank could stand it no longer, and simply went forward. "It was not just the technique . . . It was Christ. I was conscious of Him".

Graham remembers: "I simply stood up and walked forward. I showed little emotion outside and I shed no tears, and I felt like a hypocrite when I saw so many around me who were crying. Then without warning all my worries vanished and I was filled with a deep sense of joy and peace."

Standing before the altar while the evangelist pronounced the benediction, Billy had one last rebellious thought. "I'll bet it doesn't last", he said to himself. When he reached home his parents were overjoyed. They knelt together on the kitchen floor and prayed.

Next morning, he recalls, his room was flooded with the brightest sunlight he had ever seen. He walked to the window and looked out. The sky, the trees, the fields and all things seemed changed. The foliage seemed so much greener that he inspected it with special care. Still not trusting his eyes, he glanced at the flowers blooming in his mother's neat beds. Their colors were almost painfully bright. Their beauty, he thought, was created just for him. This is a not uncommon experience in those who have been "converted", e.g., Dwight Moody, who awakened the next day after his conversion to find everything brighter than before.

From then on, everyone noticed that he was changed. He was quieter, more thoughtful, kinder. He became aware of a new way of looking at things, new standards, new aims.

When he finished high school, his mother wanted

him to attend a Christian college, and he was sent to Bob Jones College, in Cleveland, Tennessee. The regime there was hard, the discipline severe and excessively restrictive, and the academic benefit not notable. Billy left after one semester, for Florida Bible Institute, outside of Tampa. This college, though not accredited either, was a more humane place and Billy found it congenial.

It was not a liberal arts college, nor was it a seminary, but aimed at a thorough grounding in the English Bible, with courses in related subjects: Greek, church history, missions, hermeneutics and pastoral theology. It was a small school, less than a hundred, which made possible a great deal of individual instruction from some excellent teachers. Billy also had the opportunity of meeting many well known evangelists who lectured there, especially during the summer months at Bible conferences held on the campus.

But still there was something missing. Billy had been converted, he wanted to know the Bible, but as he says, "I was still carefree, happy-go-lucky. I didn't amount to much". He sensed something wrong, something indecisive in his life, some lack of dedication. He felt an unmistakable call to be a preacher, yet felt himself unequipped and too poorly educated. He seemed to be drifting. One night in March 1938 he wrestled with this problem as he walked around the golf course adjoining the school, and finally solved it. "I remember getting on my knees and saying, 'O God, if you want me to preach, I will do it!' Tears streamed down my cheeks as I made this great surrender to become an ambassador for Jesus Christ".

His mind was now made up, and his direction was clear. He was pointed straight for the ministry, full time work for the Lord. He had a goal firmly in mind. The first thing he needed was a broader education. So he entered Wheaton College, Illinois, an accredited institution, as a major in anthropology. This 22-year-old freshman, his fellow students quickly saw, was older not only in years but in maturity, not a youth now but a man, with a purpose and dedication in life. He had already received appointment as a Baptist minister by the St. John's Association at Peniel, Florida, having been baptized, with his parents' approval, as a Southern Baptist.

At Wheaton he met Ruth Bell, attractive, intelligent, mature, and thoroughly Christian daughter of a Presbyterian medical missionary. They seemed eminently suited to each other, and were married in August 1943. His first pastorate after graduation was Western Springs, Illinois. In a short time his church was sponsoring a weekly radio program, with Graham preaching and George Beverly Shea, later part of his evangelistic team, singing. Later he took part in the Youth For Christ rallies that were sweeping the country at that time. He soon became vice-president of Youth For Christ International, and travelled all over the country and abroad. There were an amazing number of meetings, 360, in the British Isles from October 1946 to March 1947.

In December 1947 he finally yielded to the insistent urgings of Dr. William Bell Riley, founder and first president of Northwestern Schools in Minneapolis, and became Dr. Riley's successor as president. The institution was an amalgam of a liberal arts college, a Bible college, and a seminary. Billy had to be part-time president, delegating a great deal of authority to trusted subordinates and continuing his preaching. After four years it became evident that he could not continue both as president of the school and full-time evangelist, even though the institution had made notable progress under his presidency. It was clear where his main interest lay, so in February 1952 he resigned the presidency for full-time evangelism. By now his apostolate in this field had grown sensationally. After the highly successful crusade in Los Angeles in 1947 and the publicity given him by the Hearst newspapers, he was nationally prominent.

Graham as a Fundamentalist

Graham is identified with conservatism in theology, and has often been called a fundamentalist. Fundamentalism as a movement is a specifically American Protestant twentieth-century phenomenon. I say as a "movement", because as a thought-style, or a thought-set, it goes back much earlier of course, and it is not limited to the United States. Most Protestants until 100 years ago were fundamentalist without knowing it, like the man in Moliere's play who spoke prose.

As a movement it was a conscious reaction in the United States against liberal or "modernist" tendencies in theology, especially new interpretations of the traditional confessions and creeds and new interpretations of Scripture based on historical investigation and literary and form criticism. The movement began independently in various denominations and cut across denominational lines, pitting Presbyterian against Presbyterian and Baptist against Baptist.

From 1910 to 1912 two wealthy brothers in Los Angeles, Milton and Lyman Stewart, subsidized the writing of twelve small books entitled *"The Fundamen-*

tals. A Testimony to the Truth". Written by various authors, some of them respected theologians like Benjamin B. Warfield of Princeton Theological Seminary, these books set forth five points as fundamental: (1) the literal inerrancy and infallibility of the Bible, (2) the virgin birth and full deity of Christ, (3) the physical resurrection of Christ, (4) the atoning sacrifice of his death for the sins of the world, (5) his second coming in bodily form to preside at the Last Judgment. These books were mailed free of charge to pastors, missionaries, theology students and church workers, a total distribution of some three million copies.

The Stewart brothers also founded the Los Angeles Bible Institute, which was to do in the Far West what the Moody Bible Institute was already doing in Chicago, training hundreds of preachers and church workers in the literal sense of the Bible. Scores of these Bible institutes or colleges sprang up at this period. They were not theological seminaries, but inter-denominational centers for the propagation of the fundamentalist interpretation of Scripture. They also issued publications and promoted Bible conferences, especially in the summer months. Every year they graduated hundreds of zealous young fundamentalists and sent them back into their various denominations.

We can distinguish doctrinal fundamentalism, an adherence to the fundamental doctrines mentioned above, from biblical fundamentalism, a literal interpretation of Scripture. The two, of course, are closely connected. Biblical fundamentalism insists on the literal meaning of Scripture, that is, the obvious meaning, the meaning that leaps to mind when an ordinary twentieth-century man reads it. It excludes any investigation into what the author might have meant, in distinction to what he said. If Genesis says that God made man out of the slime of the earth, that means God made man out of slime or mud. "Says" and "means" are the same thing. There is no room for investigation into the language, modes of thought, modes of expression of the human authors, no historical, or literary, or form criticism. The Christian reader simply takes the Bible as the Word of God as it stands in modern English. This naturally rules out all forms of evolution, even theistic. The famous Scopes trial in Tennessee in 1926 made that abundantly clear.

Various national organizations were formed to promote the fundamentalist cause, the most important of them being the American Council of Christian Churches, founded by Carl McIntire in 1941; the National Association of Evangelicals for United Action, established in 1942; and the Youth for Christ International, in 1943. The McIntire group and the National Association of Evangelicals (NAE) both had as their principal purpose welding the independent churches not in sympathy with modernism into a federation that would rival the already established Federal Council of Churches, since 1950 called the National Council of Churches.

Billy Graham, as previously noted, was vice-president of Youth for Christ International. He was also in the 1950's extremely active in the NAE, and in 1952 delivered an important address to their national convention. In it he called for an ecumenical movement, not a movement for organizational unity, but a "spiritual ecumenical movement of all born-again believers". It was a call to all "orthodox" Christians who believe in the traditional doctrines of Christianity to unite: "It is time for action. It's time for an offensive in

Revival". There is no doubt that Graham is the leader in the United States of the conservative "orthodox" Protestants in all the major denominations, and a leader also of the movement throughout the world, as was pointed out earlier when speaking of his initiative in promoting the World Evangelical Congress in 1967.

The title is important. Today the more sophisticated and aware of the fundamentalists prefer to call themselves evangelicals. The extremist McIntire group, a rival to the NAE within the conservative camp, has declined in importance and today has little real influence.

But the evangelicals have. This influence has been strengthened since 1955 by the fortnightly review *Christianity Today*, founded by Graham, his father-in-law Nelson Bell, and a few others. He saw the need for a "strong, hard-hitting, intellectual magazine" which would propose the evangelical view as strongly and as intelligently as *The Christian Century*, edited by Reinhold Niebuhr, did the liberal. The magazine, now far surpassing in circulation *The Christian Century*, seems to be achieving its purpose. A typical issue, March 29, 1968, contains a discussion of the evidence for the Resurrection by the dean of law faculty of the University of London, an account of his conversion by C.S. Lewis, a discussion of Christ's teaching on rebirth by Graham himself, an article by Charles Malik, former president of the General Assembly of the United Nations, some well written editorials, including one defending biblical creationism against naturalistic evolution. The review is not a house organ of the Graham Evangelistic Association, but an independent publication, although it clearly proclaims the evangelical point of view.

In what sense then is Billy Graham a fundamentalist? He answers in his own words: "What do you mean by a fundamentalist? Do you mean by that, someone who believes God dictated the Bible to certain men as if they were dictaphones, and had no part in the matter, except insofar as they recorded the words of God? If so, then I am certainly not a fundamentalist. If on the other hand you mean by a fundamentalist one who believes the great fundamental truths of the Bible and man's need of a savior, then I certainly am".

"There are so many shades of fundamentalism", he wrote in 1956, "and so many shades of liberalism, it is increasingly difficult to point to a man and say he is a 'liberal' or he is a 'fundamentalist' without qualifying explanations. If by *fundamentalist* you mean 'narrow', 'bigoted', 'prejudiced', 'extremist', 'emotional', 'snake-handler', 'without social conscience',—then I am definitely not a fundamentalist. However, if by *fundamentalist* you mean a person who accepts the authority of the Scriptures, the virgin birth of Christ, the atoning death of Christ, His bodily resurrection, His second coming and personal salvation by faith through grace, then I am a fundamentalist. However, I much prefer being called a 'Christian' ".

It is clear that Graham is avoiding extremism. He is a "neo-fundamentalist". He clearly opts for doctrinal fundamentalism. What about his biblical fundamentalism? The following quotations will give a fairly clear idea:

I don't think there is any conflict at all between science and the Scriptures. I think we have misinterpreted the Scriptures many times and have tried to make the Scriptures say things they weren't meant to say. The Bible is not a book of science,—the Bible is a book of redemption. Of course I accept the creation story. I do

believe that God did create the Universe. I believe He
created Man; whether it came by . . . a process, and
at a certain point He took this being and made him a
living soul or not, does not change the fact that God did
create man.

I personally believe that it is (easier) to accept the statement that God breathed upon man and he became a living soul (than) to accept the claim that it started with
some protoplasm and went on up through the evolu-
tionary process. In either case, it is by faith, and which-
ever way God did it, makes no difference as to what
man is and what man's relationship to God is.

The Bible is written by about forty writers over a
period of some 1600 years. It comprises sixty-six books
and they are all concerned with one subject. Think of it,
the great theme from one end of the Bible to the other
is redemption, God's love for the human race, God
redeeming man and bringing man back to Himself after
man had rebelled against his Maker. That is what the
Bible is all about.

Then he goes on to state that the Bible agrees with
science and science agrees with the Bible. There is no
contradiction.

In commenting on a hymn called "Ivory Palaces",
he says: "We do not propose that heaven actually consists of ivory palaces. This is merely the oriental imagery which is used to try and describe the beauty of our
Lord's home when He departed to live among men on
earth". This is a change from his earlier literalism, by
which he even specified the dimensions of heaven, as
1,600 miles long, 1,600 miles wide, and 1,600 miles
high.

Here is another example of his scriptural interpretation:

Whether there is literal fire in hell or not, all these are descriptions of God's hatred for sin and they portray a Bible truth . . . If there is no fire in hell, then God is using symbolic language to indicate something far worse. Certainly no words in any language of the world can describe the awfulness and the horribleness of spending age after age without God, without hope, without light, "where the fire is never quenched and the worm dieth not".

We would say then that Graham is not a biblical fundamentalist in the sense of being a literalist. He does however generally favor that interpretation of the Bible that is commonly called literal, unless common sense and/or clear evidence demands otherwise. This condition is important, and leaves the way open to the adoption of interpretations based on sound biblical scholarship. In this matter Graham has grown with the years and quietly relinquished some earlier extremist positions, although it must be admitted that he views most biblical scholarship with a rather suspicious and skeptical eye.

At one period in his life, a few months before the Los Angeles crusade in 1947, he was beset with doubts and difficulties about the inerrancy and infallibility of Scripture. A close friend, Charles Hamilton, maintained that a doctrine taught by the Bible was intellectually untenable, and Graham replied that when he preached from the Bible as God's Word, his preaching had power and men were changed and radiant. The friend rejected this pragmatic argument, and Graham became confused and unable to answer the arguments. After agonizing over the problem for several months, Graham finally came to the conclusion that he couldn't answer all the objections from human reason, that he

had to simply take on faith that God did in fact inter-
vene in human history and the Bible was the record, set
down by human but inspired authors, of these interven-
tions.

He characteristically resolved the problem by reading the Bible more and praying more: "O God, I cannot prove certain things. I cannot answer some of the
questions Chuck is raising and some of the other people
are raising, but I accept this Book by faith as the Word
of God". From that time on he had no more hesitation.
From then on a standard, stock phrase he uses in all his
preaching is, "The Bible says. . ."

Graham does this for two reasons: (1) He is not an
apologist, but an evangelist; he simply proclaims the
message. He does not attempt to lay the groundwork
for the message with apologetic or explanatory arguments such as the reasonableness of a revelation, or
other "motives of credibility". He has no time for this
in his sermons. He thinks his time must be taken up entirely with simply proclaiming the message. (2) Graham
has found from experience, he says, that people want to
be told authoritatively that this is so, not be given arguments *pro* and *con* why this may be so or may not be
so. "The world longs for finality and authority. It is
weary of theological floundering and uncertainty. Belief
exhilarates people, doubt depresses them".

This attitude toward the Bible is combined with
doctrinal fundamentalism, strict orthodoxy in the "fundamentals of the faith". His own stand on these matters is embodied in the Youth For Christ creed, adopted in 1945: "We believe the Bible to be the inspired, the
infallible, the authoritative word of God . . . that
there is one God, eternally existent in three persons,
Father, Son and Holy Spirit . . . we believe in the

deity of our Lord Jesus Christ, in his virgin birth, in his sinless life, in his miracles, in his vicarious and atoning death through his shed blood, in his bodily resurrection, in his ascension to the right hand of the Father and his personal return to glory and power".

Graham then is strongly orthodox in the traditional sense, in what he does affirm. He leaves some doctrines unaffirmed, saying nothing about the sacraments and little about the church. These two doctrines in his thinking are true (in a sense to be determined) but they are not central to his preaching. They are not basic to the idea of a personal encounter by faith with Jesus Christ as personal Savior. In this, Graham is following the line of one of his predecessors in revivalism, Charles Grandison Finney: "The true Philosophy of promoting and consummating an excitement and publick action upon any subject is to confine the publick mind to *a point* . . . Revivals of religion afford almost endless illustration of this. Introduce Baptism, Election, or any other doctrine that does not bear on the question of immediate acceptance of Christ and you either Kill or retard the work".

Graham is uncompromising in proclaiming his orthodox creed. In his earlier career he was uncompromising also in demanding that anyone connected with his crusades subscribe to them clearly and without reserve. But he found that by taking this stand, he could not gain entry into many cities where a large proportion of the ministers were of liberal tendencies. And if the ministerial association was not in wholehearted support of a Graham crusade, it had little chance for success. Consequently Graham revised his policy and accepted sponsorship of the ministerial associations, even where some, or even many, ministers did not accept these fundamentals of his faith. This was the only way he could preach to big crowds, at least in the large cities. He justifies this present policy by saying that this practice has never led him to compromise, or to dilute his message in the least, that he will preach the same message no matter who sponsors him.

He strongly denounces those who in his mind water down the pure Gospel message and the truths of Christianity. He speaks bluntly about the lack of faith in some theological schools and some seminaries, and has openly and strongly taken issue with liberal churchmen like the late Bishop James Pike and Bishop J.A.T. Robinson over their dilution of the faith.

But for even his limited concessions to liberals he is fiercely attacked from the other side by old-line conservatives like Carl McIntire and John Rice (editor of *The Sword of the Lord*) who reproach him for his association with men of false beliefs. Other conservatives such as Erroll Hulse point out that in his crusades he is turning over his "inquirers" for instruction and counsel to ministers lacking in Christian belief.

This last is a real difficulty, and Graham seems conscious of it and apparently tries to solve it partially in some of the printed material emanating from his headquarters in Minneapolis, which exhorts his "inquirers" to join a church "where Christ is preached".

As for what is called "the social Gospel", Graham's position is clear. Taking this term to mean that the church should concern itself, or at least that Billy Graham in his preaching should concern himself, with the temporal lot of man, he wants none of it. He consistently takes the position that the evangelist's task is to preach salvation, a right relationship with God in Christ, not to reform society, and this he says is the

Church's task also. He says you cannot reform society unless you reform men. Sin is the basic cause of evil in the world, and you must eradicate sin in individual men in order to eradicate evil in society.

For this he has been taken to task, notably by Reinhold Niebuhr. Graham has answered politely by simply reaffirming his contention that it is useless to try to reform society without reforming individuals.

Even Niebuhr has had to admit that Graham's record on Negro rights has been excellent. A Southerner, brought up in Carolina, where segregation was regarded as God's law and some of his teachers quoted the Bible to prove it, Graham has consistently denounced racial discrimination. Since 1950, before the Supreme Court decision, he has refused to speak before segregated audiences, and has quietly integrated his own staff.

He does not make racial tolerance, or interracial friendship or love a condition or prerequisite or test for conversion, as Niebuhr wanted him to. But he thinks that conversion to Christ will bring with it a real love of men of all races. "The race question will not be solved by demonstrations in the streets but in the hearts of both negro and white . . . There must be genuine love to replace prejudice and hate. This love can be supplied by Christ, and only by Christ".

Graham then is in the tradition of what we can call, for want of a better term, pietistic evangelicalism. We call it evangelicalism because it professes to be based directly on the *evangelium*, the Gospel, the Bible, as distinct from "theology". We call it pietistic because it emphasizes the side of the will and affections rather than the intellect. It is a long tradition in Christianity reaching back through the classical American revivalists Jonathan Edwards, Finney and Moody to Wesley, Franke and Spener. We could, with some qualifications, go on back to Francis of Assisi, Bernard and Anselm, and even to Ignatius of Antioch and Paul of Tarsus. At any rate it was part of the air that Graham breathed in his youth. In the South it is called "heart religion", as distinct from "head religion". The idiom of pietism was the everyday idiom: "being under conviction", "meeting the Lord Jesus", "giving your heart to Christ". We have seen two conversions in his family. It was assumed that a person reared properly sooner or later would become converted, either in a crisis-type conversion or in the more gradual type that we shall note later. Being religious meant a dedication that was wholehearted, in the literal sense. It was only natural then that Graham should devote himself to making people religious in that way, to the work of conversion.

In fact, it is impossible to understand Billy Graham unless you understand his ideas on conversion, on what he calls "decision for Christ". "Decision for Christ" is the key to Graham's thought, his whole mental framework, the explanation of why he does what he does. This is why a large part of this book is precisely on this facet of the complex Graham phenomenon.

But if "decision for Christ" is the key to Graham's thought and activity, the "crusade" is for him the instrument *par excellence* of the "decision for Christ." So we will deal with the crusade first.

3. Conversion from the Outside:
The Crusade

The Organization of a Crusade

Billy Graham says "Evangelism essentially is confronting a person with Christ". The purpose of a crusade is to present as many people as possible with the claims of Christ. He gives as a definition of the work of an evangelist the classic one of the Archbishop of Canterbury's Committee of 1918: "To evangelize is so to present Christ Jesus in the power of the Holy Spirit that men shall come to put their trust in God through Him, to accept Him as their Saviour and serve Him as their King in the fellowship of His Church". His predecessors, Finney, Moody, Sunday and others, developed techniques to attract large crowds and to hold their attention and interest. Graham has improved these techniques, has refined and adapted them, eliminating whatever does not fit in with the modern taste, and has developed some new techniques to a high degree of perfection.

He never studied Finney's classic textbook on the subject, *Revivals of Religion*, until after he had been preaching a number of years. As he himself says, "When I began my ministry of evangelism over twenty-five years ago I had not read a single book on the subject of conversion. However, I had experienced conversion myself when but a young, rebellious student of sixteen".

Yet, almost from the beginning his method of organizing a crusade was essentially what it is today. By the late forties, especially through the experience gained in England in 1946-47, he and his associates had formulated certain operational policies which, it was soon found, guaranteed success: (1) cooperation by the city's ministerial association, (2) involvement in the campaign by many church congregations, (3) an unprecedented use of printing, publicity and advertising, (4) the earnest use of consecrated music to prepare restless souls, (5) the supplications of countless Christians on their knees in prayer, (6) the simple Gospel message, adorned with Gospel texts, geared to the times.

Of course it is important that the ministerial associations cooperate. If they do not, and on a broad scale, the chances for the success of the crusade are diminished. The people will usually cooperate to some extent even if the ministers are lukewarm about the crusade, but maximum results will not generally be felt unless the ministers are very active. Further, the ministers themselves must take an active part afterward in "servicing" those who make "decisions for Christ". They must counsel and instruct them, and give them special care and attention after the crusade is finished, if the fruits of the crusade are not to be lost.

Hundreds of workers, even thousands in a large crusade, are needed to do clerical work, to usher, to act as counsellors, to sing in the choir, to man telephones, to tack up placards, to distribute handbills, etc., etc. For a large crusade such as London preparations start two years ahead. For an ordinary crusade a preparatory period of nine to twelve months is normal. A skeleton staff is sent in, which rents an office and begins to recruit and organize all the people who are necessary to make the crusade a success. Hundreds of people for instance are enlisted to visit each home in the area with an invitation to come to the crusade. Organizing prayer groups is another large task. In Anaheim, California, for example, 8,300 groups of about ten women each prayed for the success of the crusade.

In Operation Andrew, so named because it was Andrew who brought his brother Simon Peter to Christ, each active church member is asked to bring an unchurched member. Transportation is arranged by bus to obviate the parking problem and give a sense of community to the group.

Counsellors have to be trained, for they are of capital importance when the inquirer, in response to the "invitation", "comes forward" to indicate that he has made his "decision for Christ". These counsellors must go through a training course in a class that meets once a week for six weeks. They are schooled in appropriate Bible texts which will support the inquirer's decision, and an attempt is made to prepare them to answer any doubts and difficulties the inquirer might have. Their number has to be considerable, for the aim is to have one counsellor for every inquirer who comes forward, although in fact this aim is not always realized. The counsellor evaluates the spiritual condition of the inquirer, making a judgment on his state of mind, his motivation, his sincerity, and then assists him with appropriate advice, and especially biblical support. These counsellors are supervised by "advisors", whose function is twofold: (1) interview the inquirer after the counsellor has seen him, to make sure the right advice was given, and (2) solve any problem that remains which the counsellor was not able to solve. There is one advisor for every ten counsellors.

A cross-section of counsellors has to be prepared—young, old, student, white-collar, blue-collar, professional—to correspond to the inquirers who will come forward, since the ideal is to match up a teen-age counsellor with a teen-age inquirer, a professional-class counsellor with a professional-class inquirer, and so on.

Then there are the ushers, who also take up the offering, and the choir, and the "co-workers", as they are called, who do all sorts of odd jobs, like typing, stuffing envelopes, processing decision cards, acting as runners to get the cards from the field or arena to the office, and doing whatever else needs to be done.

All this is an immense problem in logistics. It is all done according to a blueprint that in its broad outlines began to take form in 1946-47, was hammered into shape in London in 1954 and has been used with but slight modifications ever since. This organization plan has been tested time and again, and refined to perfection. Its merit is the pragmatic one that it works, and the local people are usually willing enough to follow the blueprints and procedure manuals that have produced such success elsewhere. When they agree to sponsor the crusade it is understood that they will work according to these procedures.

There is of course a great effort at publicity. All the media are used: press, radio, TV, magazine articles and interviews, billboards, posters, handbills. For the 1970 New York crusade, the subway cars and the stations were adorned with large posters showing Graham's smiling face and the simple announcement, "Billy's Back". The organization aims at a "peaking" of interest just a few days before the crusade, because to "peak" prematurely would be ineffective.

A special effort is made to attract youth, and there

are "Youth Nights" when the program is aimed specifically at them, with speakers who appeal especially to young people. Thus in the New York crusade, Paul Crane, football player on the New York Jets, gave a "testimony". Another was Nicky Cruz, who was billed on the program by an enthusiastic copy-writer as a former "hardened gang leader of the notorious Mau-Mau's, considered to be the most dangerous large gang in New York City. While still in his early teens, he was guilty, though not convicted, of sixteen brutal stabbings". Nicky movingly told the crowd how Christ had changed him from a certified juvenile delinquent to a convinced and apostolic Christian.

Music plays an important part in the conversion process. (What follows here is from personal observation on three different evenings at Shea Stadium, Long Island, New York, in June 1970.) While the crowd is filing into the large stadium, the choir of 3,000 is "warming up" by rehearsing. These are members of scores, even hundreds, of church choirs in the greater New York area. They are singing the moving songs so much a part of the religious sentiment of the people in the audience, "All Hail the Power of Jesus' Name", "Blessed Assurance", "A Mighty Fortress Is Our God", and so on. These familiar strains turn the atmosphere of an athletic stadium into something more reverent. They also induce an air of eager expectation.

"Decision for Christ"—"Coming Forward"

The crowd filing in is happy, well ordered, rather quiet, but not subdued; a cross-section of "middle-America". There are some beards and beads, but most wear that scrubbed, apple-pie look so often associated with "the typical American", and so often described as "wholesome". There are quite a few blacks and browns, and a whole section of Spanish-speaking. Everybody is polite, friendly and good humored, many carrying Bibles, as they have been asked to do.

Promptly at the appointed time, 7:45, on the dot, enter Billy Graham and the speakers and singers. They proceed to the large platform which has been set up between the pitcher's mound and second base, where already many platform guests are seated.

Cliff Barrows, Graham's dynamic and personable song leader and master of ceremonies, opens the program by leading the choir in "Praise Ye the Lord of Hosts". The 3,000 voices, singing in four parts, attack with precision and sing with verve and competence. Then a minute of silent prayer, with the 25,000 people in the stadium all standing with bowed heads. The silence is reverent, impressive. Then, directed by Barrows, the whole stadium, still standing, sings "All Hail the Power of Jesus' Name", after which a minister from the local committee leads a prayer.

Next, George Beverly Shea, the "beloved gospel singer", alternates with the choir in singing "How Great Thou Art". His deep rich baritone is expressive and breathes reverence. It is a prayer, not a performance. There is no applause.

Then comes a brisk two-minute welcome by the chairman of the local committee. Then Billy, handsome in his powder-blue suit, welcomes the crowd briefly and with practiced adroitness, telling a couple of moderately humorous stories which the crowd receives with gratitude. Graham then introduces Anita Bryant, a TV personality and singer, a glamorous redhead in a green dress. She sings "He Lives" in a throaty throbbing style, with a tear in her voice, almost a sob.

Next comes the business part of the meeting. Roger Hull, general chairman, tells of the total budget of $500,000 and the present shortage of $200,000. He hopes everybody here tonight will contribute something, and that some will put in more than just five or ten dollars and will feel moved to use the blank check that is detachable from the program. The ushers pass small plastic buckets up and down among the seated people. Meanwhile the organ keeps playing softly. It is all in good taste and to this observer for one it seems decently restrained, as well as deft and effective.

After a few routine announcements the whole stadium rises and sings "Blessed Assurance", followed by Bev Shea singing a solo, "Somebody Bigger Than You or I". Cliff Barrows then recommends warmly a new translation of the Pentateuch, *The Living Books of Moses.* He asks no money: they'll send it to you. He then presents Anita Bryant again and she gives a "testimony" of her faith in Christ, tells how she was saved when she was only eight years old and asked for Baptism. She has two points to make: (1) girls, keep your virginity until marriage, and (2) trust the Lord, even in almost impossible situations, as she did seventeen months ago, when she was having a difficult time in childbirth and the doctors wanted to take her twins to save her life; but she refused and the Lord saved all three.

Then, after one hour of these preliminaries at 8:45, Billy Graham comes on for his sermon. The preliminaries on subsequent nights did not take as long as on the opening night, herein described, when so many announcements had to be made and greetings given by various people.

Graham opened by asking everybody to pray, silently. He then preached on a text from the twenty-fourth chapter of Joshua: "Choose today whom you wish to serve. I and my house are going to serve the living God" (*Jos* 24:15).

To paraphrase the substance of his sermon, he noted that we have a deep need of salvation . . . we feel lonely . . . loneliness is the number one problem in New York . . . Salvation depends not on our own good works, or our own virtue, but on the blood of Christ. But we have to want to be saved . . . Do we want God for our father, or the devil? There is increasing devil worship today in Europe and in the United States . . . There really is a devil, and really is a hell, if you believe in the truthfulness of Jesus Christ, who spoke of it so many times and warned us against it. So these are our choices, God or the devil, heaven or hell. Choose you this day . . . It is urgent: this day. Dismas, the thief on the cross; "this day thou shalt be with me in Paradise" . . . Bartimeus, this day . . . The astronauts had to come to a quick decision on Apollo XIII, right away, no delay.

I was surprised at the lack of oratorical pyrotechnics. Undoubtedly this was largely because I was mistakenly expecting a great play upon emotion, but it was not entirely due to this. One can characterize the emotional content of the sermon as emotion clearly present, but restrained, low-keyed, under control.

Graham talked about 25 minutes before giving the invitation. He asked people to make their "decision for Christ" and to demonstrate this publicly by com-

ing forward to the platform while their friends and
relatives waited. Immediately a large group arose
and came forward. One had to keep in mind that most
of these were not inquirers, but counsellors, moving up
to be in position to counsel those who would come forward. But the effect on anyone who was wavering or
just thinking about coming forward must have been
very encouraging, if he thought all those people were
inquirers. The invitation lasted about 15 minutes.
Graham would talk, then pause, then talk a little more,
then pause, and so on. A typical invitation follows,
transcribed *verbatim* from a tape-recording made on a
night subsequent to the one described above. Even
though there are a few gaps, the transcription captures
the mood of the event:

Christ rose from the dead, He's alive, He's coming
back, we've been set free and thank God for the example of His life . . . Do you know Christ? Have you
received Him in your heart? You say, what do I have to
do to receive Him? You have to be willing to repent of
your sins and that means change your life and say, "I
am going to trust Him as my only God . . . He will be
my Savior . . ." "As many as received Him to them
He gave the power to become the sons of
God". . . You can't come with your mind alone, you
have to come with your heart . . . And you believe.
Simply by faith you come and He receives you, He forgives you, He changes you . . .

You young people searching for purpose and meaning
in your life, searching for a flag to follow and a song to
sing, come to Christ . . . Fathers and mothers, with
sin in your lives, of the past, that has never been forgiven, you come . . . You may be Catholic or Protestant or Jewish, or you may not have any religion. Whoever you are, whatever you are, I am going to ask you
to come, and if you are with friends or relatives, they

will wait, or if you have come on a bus . . . But I want you to come out of your seats, by the hundreds . . . Just get up and come, and after you have all stopped, I am going to say a word to you and a prayer with you, give you some literature, and you can go back and join your friends . . . This is a simple act of repentance and opening up your hearts . . .

I must ask no one to leave the stadium . . . please, no one to leave . . . This is a holy moment . . . But all over the stadium, hundreds of you get up and come, men, women, young people everywhere. The voice of the spirit of God is talking to you . . . You get up and come . . . There is still time for you to come; this is your moment and your hour . . .

Before God say yes to Christ, and receive Him as your Lord and Savior . . . We're going to wait and ask no one to leave . . . This is a holy moment . . . Many are coming. Just keep coming while I am talking, and you can listen while you come. Many people are coming down almost every aisle . . . Keep on coming. You come tonight not to me, but to Christ. I have no power, but Christ does have power. He has the power to forgive all your faults. Whatever you have done that is wrong, whatever you have done in your life, he will forgive you. That's what He did on the cross, He died and took your place on the cross . . . and God says, "I love you; I love you so much I gave My Son Jesus Christ, to die for you", and He gives Himself totally and completely to you as if you were the only person in all the world. That's how much He loves you. He loves you so much He would die on the cross and stay on the cross for you . . .

That's the good news of the Gospel, that's what the word Gospel means, good news. God loves you, He forgives you, because of Christ, not because you are good, not because you deserve it, but because of Christ . . .

Now, from tonight on, there are four things that are very important. First, read your Bible every day. This helps you grow. We are going to give you a Gospel of John tonight. We are going to give you some verses to memorize, and we are going to give you a Bible-study. Finish that Bible-study, fill it out. It's so simple that a child could do it, and it is so simple that a professor at the university can also do it. So, fill it out, send it in, and we will send you another one in the mail. This helps you to grow. Then the second thing is, pray. You are God's child now. He hears you. He will answer your prayers.

Then, thirdly, witness for Christ. Witness by the way you live. Love your neighbor. Witness for Christ by coming to the meeting tomorrow afternoon and bringing friends with you . . . Witness by going to church. That's the fourth thing. Get into a church where Christ is waiting, and get to work for Christ through the church. You say, "But I don't like the church". Someone asked an old lady why she went to church, and she said, "I go to church to show which side I'm on". If you don't like the church, go at least to show which side you're on. And if the church is not what it ought to be, you can help it to be what it ought to be.

So I'm going to ask now that we bow our heads in prayer . . . every head bowed . . . (out loud): "Oh God, I am a sinner. I am sorry for my sins. I am willing to turn from my sins, to receive Christ the Savior, by professing His love. From this moment on I want to follow Him and share with Him in the fellowship of His church. In Christ's name, Amen".

Some of your counsellors may have to talk to four or five people, because there are so many people . . . We are going to have another prayer and after that the counsellors will say a word, and all of you here, every person here tonight, will consider it your responsibility to come back tomorrow afternoon.

How important is "coming forward" and thus making a public commitment? Very important, according to Graham. He lays great stress on it: "Certainly this act is not necessary for conversion. However it has sound psychological and biblical basis". He gives biblical examples: Moses in Exodus (32:26) after the destruction of the golden calf, saying "Who is on the Lord's side? Let him come unto me". And Joshua (*Jos* 24:15) appealing to Israel to make a definite decision and commitment: "Choose you this day whom you will serve"; and Joshua then memorializing in writing and by a memorial stone the choice of the people for Yahweh. Ezra (10:5) called upon the people to swear publicly to carry out his reforms. On Pentecost 3,000 made a public commitment for the Lord in one day.

In addressing 5,800 delegates to the Seventh Baptist Youth Conference, he does not take their commitment for granted but stresses open confession, even to this supposedly dedicated audience. He asks three things: repentance, receiving Christ by faith as Lord and Savior, and receiving him openly and publicly. "If you will not confess me publicly I will not confess you before my Father".

Only a small percentage of the audience responds to the call to come forward and make their decision for Christ. It varies from 3% to a phenomenal 13.7% on Maui, Hawaii. In the average crusade it will run from 3 to 4%. Those who come forward sign a card which indicates that they accept Jesus Christ as their Savior and Lord. They wish to enter a new phase of their lives, to change their lives in a significant way. Since 1951 Graham, with commendable restraint, calls these people "inquirers", not "converts". He sees them not as necessarily converted, as "born-again Christians", but as potentially so. There is also a space on the card for those who have already gone forward on a previous occasion and who now indicate, by a check, that they have received "assurance of salvation", and still another space for those who make a "rededication" of their lives with renewed fervor.

The Follow-Up

The inquirer is given a little packet, which contains: (1) a short note of congratulations and encouragement from Billy Graham; (2) a small decision card which he signs and will carry in his wallet as a memento and reminder of his decision; on the reverse side is the name, address and telephone number of his counsellor; (3) the Gospel of St. John in the *Living Gospels* paraphrase by Kenneth N. Taylor; (4) two simple Bible lessons, one to be done and mailed in right away, the other to be sent in only after the first lesson is corrected and returned; (5) four small memory cards, wallet size, in a carrier for frequent use. Two of the cards have Scripture texts, Jn 3:16 and I Jn 1:9, and two are lists of the books both of the Old and New Testaments, together with the number of chapters they contain and their abbreviations.

There is follow-up by the counsellor, by the minister, and by the Graham organization.

1. *Follow-Up by the Counsellor*. Within two days the counsellor is to contact the inquirer, by personal visit if possible, or if this is not possible, by telephone or letter. The purpose of this contact is to encourage the inquirer in his newly taken resolutions and good dispositions, and to check on whether he has memo-

rized Jn 3:16 and completed and mailed Bible Lesson Number 1.

2. *Follow-Up by the Minister.* One of the bits of information learned from the inquirer is his religious affiliation and background, together with the address of a particular church within that denomination. This last is supplied, if necessary, by a large staff of volunteer researchers, working that same night with city and church directories. The minister's name, address and telephone number are also noted, either by the individual inquirer or by the research staff. The inquirer's name, address and telephone number are then typed out on special business forms that evening by a large staff of volunteers who will work until 2 a.m. if necessary, and mailed to the minister that same night with the request that he (1) visit the person as soon as possible, (2) offer encouragement and counsel as needed, and (3) complete and return the report form within one week. On the report form there is only one box to be checked: "I have visited and encouraged this person". For comments there are blank spaces. It is presumed that the minister will cooperate. If he is slow, there is a carbon copy which is sent, a short time after the week is up, exactly the same form, with the request that he fill it out and return it "as soon as possible". If this does not produce results, another identical copy is sent out with the notation that if there is no report forthcoming by a certain date the inquirer's name will be turned over to another minister. One of these three steps usually produces the desired effect.

A certain number of inquirers do not answer the question about religious affiliation and background or preference. Usually the reason is that they have had little or no contact with ministers or clergymen nor interest in any particular church congregation. Where then to assign them? This is a delicate question, since it might involve proselytizing, and could cause professional jealousy among the ministers, and thus seriously damage the work of the crusade. To handle this question a committee of ministers of various congregations and denominations reviews all the cases in this undecided category and assigns them as fairly and objectively as possible to some particular minister on the basis of proximity to the inquirer, or proven facility in dealing with this particular type of inquirer, or some other basis.

It is interesting to note that there is no follow-up on Roman Catholics. This is because the Roman Catholic Church does not actively participate in Graham's crusades, although the late Cardinal Cushing met with Billy and gave public support to the crusade when it came to Boston. Active participation necessarily includes participation of the clergy who must undertake the task of counseling and giving special attention to the inquirers who are harvested from the crusade.

In the follow-up room in Shea Stadium in June 1970 I saw a thick packet of decision cards designated "No follow-up". These were "Catholic and Cultists". (The Cultists were roving Pentecostals with no fixed abode, snake-handlers, etc.). There is no follow-up on these cases. They are simply dropped. I was told that the percentage of Catholic decisions for Christ reached almost 20% of the whole. That was, it must be remembered, in New York, where the percentage of Catholic population is high, especially in relation to the Protestant population. In 1966, in London 10% of the inquirers were Catholic on the night of June 1. This percentage dropped later, but several score were among the inquirers every night. About 80% of these wished to remain Roman Catholics.

3. *Follow-Up by the Graham Organization.* (1) Each inquirer who comes forward receives a year's subscription *gratis* to *Decision* magazine, in which many of the articles are aimed at strengthening newly found faith. (2) The Follow-Up Department of the Billy Graham Evangelistic Association in Minneapolis undertakes to correct each Bible lesson and to mail the next lesson to the inquirer. (There are six of these lessons.) (3) The crusade organization makes every effort after the crusade to see that the inquirer is put into contact with a suitable minister and so get active in a church. Thus he will be able to gain support to live the Christian life. This is one of the main tasks undertaken by the crusade office, which typically will remain operating in a large city from six months to a year after a crusade.

The program that the individual is to follow, as preached by Graham in his sermons and by the Association in its printed material, is simple and clear. To quote from one of the pieces sent out by the organization:

This is just the beginning of a wonderful new life with Christ. Now:
1. Read your Bible every day to get to know Christ better.
2. Talk to God in prayer every day.
3. Tell others about Christ.
4. Worship, fellowship, and serve with other Christians in a church where Christ is preached.

4. Conversion from the Inside: What Really Happens?

Now that we have seen what happens externally in conversion at a crusade, we will analyze conversion more deeply, trying to see what happens, as it were, from the inside. To do this, we shall first notice how Billy Graham describes it, and into what elements he breaks it up.

Graham does not always use the same terminology, but changes it from time to time. This is not surprising. He is a preacher, talking to many different audiences, not a systematic theologian writing a careful exposition of a logical structure. So he describes conversion differently at different times, according to the needs of the particular audience he is addressing at the moment.

Thus, in a book chapter called "The New Birth", he simplifies the elements of conversion and apparently makes faith the sole requisite, using the words of Paul to the jailer in Philippi (*Acts* 16:30, 31): "Believe in the Lord Jesus Christ, and thou shalt be saved". But then he amplifies a little: "There are at least two elements in conversion, repentance and faith".

In another place he identifies conversion with repentance: "Conversion or repentance was the basic note in the call of John the Baptist . . . of Jesus . . . of the early church. There is no doubt that conversion and repentance are two ways of describing the same event". Later in the same article, he speaks of repentance and/or conversion and faith: "In fact the only way to

49

enter this Kingdom was by repentance and faith".

In a radio talk called "Christian Conversion" he says that conversion is the human side of the tremendous transformation that takes place in the divinely wrought "new birth" or "regeneration". It is simply man's turning from sin to Christ. Later, he breaks this down into different elements: (1) recognize you are a sinner, (2) recognize that Christ died and rose for you, (3) receive Christ by faith. These three elements he then combines into "receiving Christ by repentance and faith".

In another sermon, "What Is Conversion?" he says biblical conversion involves three steps, two active, one passive. In active conversion, repentance and faith are involved. Repentance is conversion viewed from its starting point, the turning from the former life. Faith indicates the objective point of conversion, the turning to God. The third, which is passive, is the new birth or regeneration.

In his very first radio sermon he said in describing conversion: "The first thing we have to do is repent, the second to receive Christ, and the third, to obey Christ. So it's repent, receive, obey".

In spite of these verbal differences, from a study of his concept of conversion in these and other sermons and writings, we can come to a harmonization and use for our purposes the terminology he favors most. It is a fair statement of his thought to say that Graham, although he sometimes identifies conversion with repentance, generally understands *repentance* as one of the elements of a broader concept of conversion. The other elements are *faith* and *rebirth*. *Repentance* and *faith* are considered as active elements (even though, as we shall see later, they have passive aspects), and *rebirth* is something passive, something done to the convert.

Let us analyze each of these three elements.

Repentance: Turning From

Graham adheres to the general biblical notion of *metanoia*, a change of mind, a change of heart for the better. He gives examples of repentance in Scripture (*Lk* 13:3-5; *Acts* 3:19, 8:22, 17:30) in which the general notion of a change of heart is clear. In each case the biblical word is *metanoia*. He notes that it is not the same as penance, i.e., the voluntary suffering of punishment for sin, or remorse, i.e., regret, or self-condemnation, which has no necessary connotation of interior change. Repentance is rather sorrow for sin and complete turning away from sin.

The basis of repentance is a vivid realization of one's need. William James, in his *The Varieties of Religious Experience*, has given a classic descriptive definition of repentance: "To be converted, to be regenerated, to receive grace, to experience religion, to gain an assurance, are so many phrases which denote the process, gradual or sudden, by which a self, hitherto divided, and consciously wrong, inferior and unhappy, becomes unified and consciously right, superior and happy, in consequence of its firmer hold upon religious realities".

James is quoted in this context because, although neglecting here the element of sorrow for sin which is a constitutive element of repentance and conversion, he does bring out very clearly the element of realization of need. One must *experience* himself as "divided and consciously wrong, inferior and unhappy", otherwise there is no possibility of repentance and hence no conversion. You must not only *be* wrong, but *feel* wrong. The Pharisee in the temple saying his self-righteous prayer is not yet ripe for conversion, although he certainly needs it. He must first be humbled, be made to feel inadequate and inferior.

This is not only a preliminary to conversion, but a prerequisite. No one is converted who is not *consciously* divided and unhappy. If he does not realize his unhappy state, he must be made to do so. Consequently Graham emphasizes this often in his preaching: there is something wrong with the world, or with America, or with man, or with each of us, according to the context of his sermon.

He often speaks of the contemporary malaise, the "angst" of modern man. We are "the death-sentence generation", all our subconscious and even conscious life overshadowed by the threat of The Bomb, with a hopelessness and a pessimism not found in any other generation. He quotes Noel Coward in a popular musical play:

> In this strange illusion,
> Chaos and confusion,
> People seem to lose their way.
> What is there to strive for,
> Love or keep alive for?

Modern man feels himself a cosmic orphan, adrift on a planet precariously balanced in space. As for life on this planet, our prisons are full to overflowing, there are not enough doctors to take care of our mental patients, there is corruption in business and political life, sexual immorality in family life and out of it, a general breakdown in the moral fabric and tone of our civilization.

He points to the example of Sweden, with no poverty and the highest standard of living in the world, but with its suicide rate among students the highest in the world; and of the Canadian honor graduate who, as he graduated from the university, tore up his diploma publicly because he said his education had not answered the basic needs of his life or explained why he must suffer and why feel guilt.

He comes back again and again to mental illness, and says that guilt is the central problem of mankind, tells us of the statement of the director of a London mental hospital that half of his patients could be dismissed if they could be assured of forgiveness. Speaking before President Johnson and many leading members of Congress on the signs preceding the coming of the Son of Man in the 25th chapter of Luke, he comments on the Greek words Luke uses: "sunoche", distress or agony, and "aporia", perplexity or bewilderment, and notes that this agony and bewilderment characterize our own age.

An outstanding mathematician came to him, ready for suicide. His problem was not financial, nor domestic, nor professional. It was an emptiness he could not explain. "He belonged to the world of the misfits, the world of the lost people". He quotes Sartre, "There is no exit from the human dilemma", and theologian John McKay to the Princeton students, "The anthropological problem is the crucial problem of our generation".

He quotes T.S. Eliot:

We are the hollow men

We are the stuffed men
Leaning together
Headpiece filled with straw . . .

He is not optimistic about man's ability to create "The Great Society" talked about by some American political figures. He replied to Walter Reuther, labor leader, who ventured the opinion that with our modern technology we were on the verge of creating a paradise on earth, "Walter, there is only one flaw, and that is human nature". And Reuther agreed, "That's the flaw".

He speaks of the belief that man is naturally good as an illusion, not gotten from the Greeks, nor from Judaism, nor from Christianity. He quotes Jeremias: "The heart is deceitful above all things and desperately wicked. Who can know it?" And Carl Jung: "All the old primitive sins are not dead but are crouching in the dark corners of our modern hearts . . . still there, and still ghastly as ever". And John, to the church at Laodicea: "Thou sayest 'I am rich, and increased with goods, and have need of nothing'; and knowest not that thou art wretched, and miserable, and poor, and blind and naked". Graham explains all this human misery by the Bible's explanation: "The Bible says the trouble with the world can be summarized simply as sin, sin in the human heart".

This human sinfulness is not just widespread; it is universal. He frequently quotes St. Paul: "All have sinned and come short of the glory of God" (*Rom* 3:23), and the Psalms: "There is none righteous, no, not one" (14:3; 53:3).

Sin for Graham began with Adam: Adam started the long history of sin; he let sin into the world. Our sin is hereditary in the sense that Adam left us a legacy of his bad example, and also in the sense that we are born with a weakened human nature, with a proneness to sin, a tendency and inclination to sin.

How all men get this way, and in precisely what way this weakness in their nature derives from Adam, Graham does not explain in any detail. He simply deals with the fact, testified to in many places in Scripture, and by the experience of the human race.

In this connection, Graham preaches repentance and conversion to all, even to those who apparently are already "saved". One of the inquirers in London was a minister, a missionary for 25 years, and "a giant in his denomination". Graham speaks of the need for conversion of Nicodemus, a leader in Israel who "fasted two days a week, spent two hours daily in prayer in the temple, tithed all his income, taught as a professor of theology in the seminary . . . and still it wasn't enough". John Wesley, even though an Anglican priest and a missionary in America for a time, still needed conversion because he felt something missing; he was not surrendered.

To sum up then, in all his strictly evangelistic sermons, that is, those aimed directly at conversion, and in many of the others as well, Graham exploits the intuition that most men have of their own inadequacy, incompleteness, division, unfulfillment, instability, unworthiness, perplexity, sinfulness. He awakens it if it is not there, and reinforces it if it is. This is an important part of his message; it is essential to conversion. To quote Dr. James Stewart of Edinburgh, "The very disillusionment of today is the raw material of the Christian hope".

Graham tries to get his audience to realize this

disillusionment very vividly, to see and see clearly that there is something wrong with them. This he calls "being under conviction". This is an expression commonly used in evangelical circles, and means the process of becoming convinced that all this is terribly true. It is in the order of intellect because it is a dawning realization, but it carries with it an emotional impact. It is very close to Newman's "real knowledge" as opposed to his "notional knowledge". It is the awakening of a sluggish or dormant conscience; the sudden, vivid awareness that we have lost our way, are wrong. It is a gift of the Holy Spirit. "Before any man can come to the cross of Christ and have his sins forgiven, he must be convicted of his sins, and that convicting work is done by the Holy Spirit upon the soul".

The indispensable element in repentance is contrition. Graham emphasizes here the notion of brokenness or being broken, quoting Psalm 34, "The Lord is nigh unto them that are of a broken heart, and saveth such as be of a contrite spirit". This contrition or "godly sorrow" is not shallow sentiment nor empty emotion; it is sincere regret over past sins and an earnest desire to walk in a new path.

The motivation for this contrition comes not only from all that we have seen above—our own sinfulness and emptiness and frustration—although this motivation is certainly strong. Another powerful motive in contrition is the love of God shown for us on Calvary. "When we stand at the cross of Calvary and see what our sins cost God, our hearts should be broken and contrite". Graham relates that on one occasion after a sermon that he wasn't satisfied with, a friend pointed out that the lack of power in the sermon was because he hadn't preached the cross. "I determined that every evangelistic sermon I preached from then on would be the cross. There's power in the cross. Paul said, 'I determined to know nothing among you save Jesus Christ and Him crucified' ''.

The redemptive death is one of the articles of Graham's orthodox creed, as we have seen, and he preaches it again and again. He typically cites the song, "Amazing love! How can it be, That Thou my Lord, Shoulds't die for me?" He devotes whole sermons to this theme, but most of his evangelistic sermons contain at least some pointed reference to the redemptive death on the cross. The cross in Graham's thought is a powerful motive for contrition. But contrition, real contrition, involves changing. If we are truly sorry for our sins, we will change our way of acting. We will turn, go a different way, change course. We will turn away from all this, to something better, immeasurably better—Jesus Christ.

Faith: Turning To

It is Billy Graham's constant theme that Jesus Christ is the answer to the woes of the world and the woes of the individual; in other words, not only the answer in general, but a personal answer to the problems of each one personally. Graham aims with his preaching to bring every person in his audience to be convinced that "Christ is my answer". Thus, to take but a few examples:

Christ offers us fulfillment, fullness, victorious Christian living. He is the answer to sorrow, to suffering, to sadness and discouragement, to guilt feelings, to loneliness. Escapism is the order of the day; escapism into pleasure, materialism, false security, etc. But Christ is the only real escape from your problems.

Christ is the life, the way, the truth. He answers the needs of our heart as life, our wills as way, our minds as truth.

"You have the problem of sin in your lives, but no matter if you've broken every one of the commandments, God can forgive you today because Jesus Christ died on the cross for your sins".

Around 70% of patients in a general hospital have psychosomatic problems; 75% of psychological problems have a religious basis. God can rid you of a sense of sin, boredom, anxiety, perplexity, loneliness, inner conflict. Faith in Christ ends uncertainty, brings joy, inward peace and love.

Christians are not fearful of death, but regard it as a friend rather than a foe. They look forward to a triumph.

The cross of Christ offers us four R's: redemption, reconciliation, regeneration, and righteousness.

To worry is universal; everybody does it. But Christ, without taking away our problems, gives us the grace and serenity to bear them in peace. Suffering of all kinds, physical and mental, is the lot of man. But in the midst of this suffering the Christian has the comforting promise of victory.

He quotes Isaiah (55:2): "Hearken diligently unto me, and eat ye that which is good, and let your soul delight itself in fatness", and asks, "Do you find what you are searching for? Are you really happy? God—Christ—can give you happiness".

So we have seen that in repentance the inquirer is brought to a vivid realization of his need in *conviction*, he is brought to *contrition*, he is brought to the point of *changing* by being confronted by the person and claims of Christ to fill his now clearly realized incompleteness. The inquirer is now at the point of "accepting Christ in faith". What does this mean?

The Object of Faith. The object of our faith is of course Christ; Christ in his historical reality. Graham insists on this last point. The Incarnation, he says, is historical fact and Christianity has its roots in the deep firm soil of history. God came right down amid the din and confusion of this world, participated in our pain, suffering, conflicts, and sorrow. "At a specific time and at a specific place, God invaded the world with his presence in the form of man". The person proposed for faith is an historical figure who lived, preached, suffered, and died in Palestine, rose from the dead, and will come again in glory to judge the living and the dead.

More precisely, the object of our faith is this historical person as *savior*. The death of Christ was a free offering of himself for the sins of men. Graham does not delve into the theology of "soteriology". He simply takes Scripture at face value that Jesus gave his life for others, that his blood was shed for all, for the remission of sins (*Mt* 26:27; *Mk* 14:24; *Lk* 22:19-20; I *Cor* 11:23-25). He does not explain precisely the mode of the atonement. He takes for granted that it was some form of vicarious atonement. "Here is the act of substitution raised to the highest degree". In some real way we are saved through his passion and death. "Man says that Christ is just a great example, but God says that Christ is the Savior of the world".

The paschal lamb whose blood was sprinkled on the doorposts of the Jews in Egypt and saved them was a type of the blood of the Lamb which delivers mankind from the slavery of sin. He quotes Hebrews (9:22), "Without the shedding of blood there is no forgiveness", Paul in I Corinthians (5:7), "Christ our Passover is sacrificed for us", and Isaiah (53:5), "He was wounded for our transgressions . . . bruised for our iniquities . . . and with his stripes we are healed".

We are to have faith not only in the suffering Christ, but also in the triumphant Christ. Graham often preaches on Christ's triumph, his resurrection and coming again in glory to judge the living and the dead.

So much for the object of our faith. How does Graham understand the act of faith?

The Act of Faith. For him it is not simply an act of the intellect, an act of assenting to a truth on the authority of God revealing. It is that of course, but much more than that. Nor is it simply an act of the will, a wish, a longing, a desire, although it is that too. Nor is it simply emotion, an affection, a sentiment, although it is this also. It is more than any one of them; it is all of them together. It is a commitment to Christ the Savior that is total, it is a surrender of self, it is a dedication that holds nothing back. It is the whole of a person, with all his faculties, abilities, capacities, turning to Christ in total self-donation.

Graham would agree with Paul Tillich's description of faith:

Faith is the state of being ultimately concerned. Man is concerned about many things. When a particular concern claims ultimacy it demands the total surrender of him who accepts this claim and it promises total fulfillment, even if all other claims have to be subjected to it or rejected in its name. Faith as ultimate concern is an act of the total personality and involves body, soul and spirit. It happens in the center of the personal life and includes all its elements, conscious and unconscious, rational and non-rational, emotion and will. Otherwise faith does not occur and compulsion takes its place.

The operative concept here is the totality of this dedication. After using examples of a certain fanatical communist, a wounded army officer in Korea who would never walk again, the faith of Abraham ready to sacrifice Isaac, and Moses choosing to suffer affliction with his people rather than enjoy the soft life of the Egyptians, he says simply "God demands all—no less".

This faith then is a complete and unconditional surrender to Jesus Christ. Graham says it involves four things: self-renunciation, reliance with utter confidence on Christ, obedience, and a changed life. It is evident that he is talking about what the classic Catholic theologians call *fides viva*, living faith, animated by charity and good works. The renunciation implies a giving up of self through a choice of Christ over sin. This is an active, personal, vital faith, not a speculative act, an assent of the intellect to a proposition.

Faith for Graham involves all the faculties. It is an assent of the mind, a choice of the will, and an engagement of the affections. He does not minimize the intellectual element of faith. In a sermon called "Facts, Faith and Feeling", he makes this very clear. Faith always implies an object. This he calls a fact. Saint Paul tells us (I *Cor* 15:1, 3, 4) that we are saved because we believe that Christ died for our sins, that he was buried, that he rose again the third day. The work of Christ is a fact, his tomb is a fact, the resurrection is a fact. We believe in facts. The facts precede our faith. "You are not called upon to believe in something that is not credible, but to believe in the fact of history that in reality transcends all history".

But faith means more than an intellectual assent to the claims of Christ. It involves the will, a decision to believe. We have to "receive what Christ has done for us". We have to surrender, and commit. These are acts of will.

Last comes emotion or feeling. This is a result of faith, as Graham sees it. The act of faith itself is not necessarily emotional at all. The Bible does not attribute any emotion to it. It simply calls it belief. But belief is an experience, not a predominantly emotional experience, but an encounter with reality. A man "is justified by faith, not feeling, by trusting the finished work of Christ on the cross, and not by bodily sensations and religious ecstasy".

This does not mean that Graham discounts feeling. We shall go into this question in more detail later on. For the present we simply note that he is saying that feeling doesn't save, faith does. Of course feeling results from faith and often accompanies it. When I understand Christ's love for me, I respond with love. There are other feelings of boldness, confidence, joy in being released from guilt, trust, love and affection for other Christians, etc. These are not the very essence of faith, but are usually involved in it.

In all this the will is the most important thing. "People can pass through mental conflicts and emotional crises without being converted. Not until they exercise the prerogative of a free moral agent and will to be converted are they actually converted. This act of the will is an act of acceptance and commitment . . . Almost the last word of the Bible is this invitation: 'And whosoever will, let him take of the water of life freely' (*Rev* 22:17). It is up to you. You must will to be saved. It is God's will, but it must become your will, too".

Rebirth

This is the third element in conversion, which Graham calls passive, the other two being repentance and faith. When the heart is opened to let Christ come in by faith, "at that precise moment the Holy Spirit performs the miracle of the new birth. You actually become a new moral creature. There comes the implantation of the divine nature. You become a partaker of God's own life. Jesus Christ, through the Spirit of God, takes up residence in your heart. . . . The converted person will love what he once hated, and hate what he once loved . . . (in regard to God) he now finds himself in a state of reverence, confidence, obedience, and devotion. . . . Before conversion there may have been gratification of the flesh. Culture and intellectual pursuits or the making of money may have been of first and supreme importance. Now righteousness and holiness of heart and living the Christian life will be placed above all other concerns, for pleasing Christ will be the only thing of real importance".

This is a *radical* change. He calls it the "needed revolution", because it is so drastic. He recalls Christ's words to Nicodemus, "Except a man be born again . . ." (*Jn* 3:3), and Ezekiel's (36:26), "A new heart also will I give you, and a new spirit will I put within you". Saint Paul calls it "being alive from the dead" (*Rom* 6:13) and being "a new creature; old things are passed away . . . all things are become new (II *Cor* 5:17). To the Ephesians Paul explained the rebirth by saying they had been "quickened", or made alive from the dead (2, 1), and Peter calls it being made "partakers of the divine nature" (II *Pt* 1:4).

Graham's fullest explanation of this regeneration is given in an essay called "The New Birth", which is a contribution to a book called *Fundamentals of the Faith*. He compares the rebirth to the larva in the cocoon emerging a butterfly; the old and the ugly are left behind and the new and beautiful come into being. The moment we are converted to Christ, several dramatic things happen, whether we are aware of them or not. First, our sins are forgiven and we are justified. This is through the redemptive death of Christ. "Throughout the New Testament we are told that the one who receives Christ as Savior also receives immediately, as a gift from God, the forgiveness of sin". But God not only forgives, he justifies. Man is actually without guilt in God's sight. "I am justified and it is just-as-if-I'd never sinned". It is like erasing a typing error on a bond paper treated with special chemicals. The erasure leaves no blemish.

Second, we are adopted, with the adoption of sons, of children (*Gal* 4:5; *Eph* 1:5). "The moment we receive Christ as Savior, we receive the divine nature of the sons of God. . . . We now have all the rights of a son".

Third, the new man is indwelt by the Spirit of God. Before the Ascension, Christ promised to send the other Comforter to abide in them (*Jn* 14:16,17). Paul reminds the Romans (8:9), "But ye are not in the flesh but in the Spirit, if so be that the Spirit of God dwell in you", and the Corinthians (I *Cor* 3:16) that they are the temple of God and the Spirit of God dwells in them.

Further, the Spirit gives us special power to work

for Christ. He produces in us the supernatural fruits of the Spirit: "love, joy, peace, long-suffering, gentleness, goodness, faith, meekness and temperance" (*Gal* 5:22, 23).

Fourth, the new man has from the Spirit strength to resist temptation. We are helpless of ourselves to resist. But the Spirit within us is powerful. Our victory is not the result of our own struggling. It is the life and activity of God within us. The new man is not perfect. He is still tempted, and he sometimes yields. He is never flawless. The element of conflict is never absent. "The flesh lusteth against the Spirit, and the Spirit against the flesh" (*Gal* 5:17). The Christian possesses a new nature, surely, but the old nature is still there too. He sometimes sins, but he hates it. He confesses his sin and is restored to the fellowship of God. He does not make a practice of sin. "The perfect Christian is the one who, having a sense of his own failure to attain, is minded to press toward the mark".

The new man has new standards. "From now on our choices are made from a new perspective and a new dimension. When we are living up to the full privileges and powers of our new life in Christ, sin loses its control over these choices and dispositions. The Christian is under the domination of Christ and consequently lives according to new standards with a new power". The new man has a new orientation—to Christ; a new motivation—God's will; a new direction—toward God; new growth—spontaneous and natural, as opposed to forced and artificial; new social concern—outside of himself, living for others.

"Thus in Jesus Christ, the new man is actually a new man . . . he is not the old man improved or made over. He is not even the old man reformed or remo-

deled, for God does not make the new out of the old,
nor put new wine in old bottles. The new man is
"Christ formed in us" (*Rom* 8:19).

The question may be raised: is this a psychological change, or does it go deeper? Is it a change of
outlook, of motivation, of orientation, or is it in the
person's very being, affecting his very nature, so that
whatever change of outlook and motivation there is, is
conceived to stem from a change in the innermost self.
(In Scholastic terms: is the change moral or ontological?)

Graham almost answers this question in so many
words: "This new man is not the product of psychological change. According to psychiatrist Ernest White,
Christian conversion 'has permanent results in the
depths of the personality and sets a man forward on the
path of sanctity. Psychological treatment can bring
about a re-arrangement of the mental and emotional
pattern, but it does not introduce a new power into the
life' ". So the new man is not the product of the psychological change, but the psychological change is
rather the product of the newness of the man. A new
power has been added to the man. In Scholastic terms,
it would seem that the person is now possessed of supernatural power, a new nature, a principle of action
therefore, enabling him to perform actions which before
were beyond his reach.

This is confirmed by the language Graham uses.
He consistently makes the point that we are talking
here about something completely new and different. He
speaks of a new heart, a new spirit, a new nature. In
nontechnical language he speaks of the impotence of
human nature, unaided by grace, to save his own soul.
Human nature needs more than a patch-up job. He uses

the example from Jeremiah in which the potter made the clay into another completely new vessel. "Jeremiah doesn't say that the Potter mended the vessel, rather that he made it again into another vessel, as seemed good to the Potter to make it". He also speaks of the ability to love others as a capacity given by God. "This change is brought about by a direct, supernatural intervention of God".

This language would indicate, I believe, that, although of course Graham does not use Scholastic terminology or put the question in these terms, what he is saying in his own terminology is that the change is not merely moral, but ontological, in the convert's very nature.

The State of Being Converted

Once a person is converted, this is only the beginning. Graham insists on this: "You have become a child of God. You have been born into His family as a baby". When he is asked if these new converts will survive, he answers that the same question could just as sensibly be asked as one looks through the heavy glass windows of a maternity ward at the newborn infants there. "The answer is: No, they will not survive—not unless for a long time they are cared for, nurtured and helped to grow".

This care of new converts is an object of special concern to Graham and his associates. Walter Smyth, Crusade Director, questioned about the difference between Graham's campaigns and those of Moody and Sunday, answered: "The big difference is our concern about what happens to a New Christian".

Graham has a formula for the survival and development of the new convert in the Christian life. It is: Bible reading, prayer, and fellowship.

First, *Bible reading.* He is personally convinced that the Bible has the answer to every human problem, simply because it is God's word to us. His preaching is Bible-based. His themes are biblical, and practically all his illustrations are drawn from the Old and New Testaments. He himself reads Scripture for at least a half-hour every day. He carries the Bible with him almost everywhere he goes, so that he can read it at odd moments.

No wonder then that he tells new converts to get a Bible as quickly as possible and start reading it, quoting Psalm 119:9: "Wherewithal shall a young man cleanse his way? By taking heed according to thy word . . . Thy word have I hid in mine heart, that I might not sin against thee". He challenges them not only to read, but to memorize portions of God's word. He reminds them of Satan's attacks, which will be more severe now that they have been converted. Satan can be overcome only with the weapons God has provided. So, they are to "take the sword of the Spirit, which is the word of God" (*Eph* 6:17). Christ, tempted by the devil, put his enemy to flight by quoting Scripture three times. This is a mighty weapon.

This is a point that is made by the Graham team not only with the new converts, but also with the ministers who are to deal with them after conversion. At the ministers' meeting in London in 1966, Dr. Ferm told them: "People converted in a crusade have an insatiable hunger for the word of God; they will not be content unless you feed them well".

Second, *prayer.* This is essential too for perseverance. He quotes Jesus, telling us to pray always (*Lk* 18, 1), telling us to ask and receive, that our joy may be full (*Jn* 16:24). Graham gives the new converts a very simple prayer: "O Father, thank You for saving my soul. I love You. In Christ's name. Amen". Soon, he says, they will be praying about everything, even in their subconscious, thus fulfilling Paul's injunction to "pray without ceasing" (I *Thes* 5:17).

Graham, himself prays frequently and regularly. He really believes in it, and apparently leads an intense prayer life. He says that any day that he leaves his room without his "quiet time with God", he looks for the devil to hit him from every angle. He insists that the power of ministry does not come from one's own ability, but from God, from the Holy Spirit, and "the Holy Spirit must give a fresh daily anointing that comes from the time you are with God".

Third, *Christian fellowship*. This too is necessary for remaining converted and growing in the Spirit. Considerable effort is expended, as we have seen, on "follow-up", on contacting the inquirer to get him active in a church. The new convert needs support and encouragement in his new and unaccustomed life. He needs counseling and advice. He needs instruction, especially in how to read the Bible with understanding. All of this supposes church membership. Graham tells the new convert that God does not intend him to live the Christian life alone; he needs to be in the fellowship of a church, and quotes Hebrews (10:25), "not forsaking the assembling of ourselves together". A live coal, separated from the others, soon dies out, but if put with other live coals, it will be a glow lasting a long time.

Included in the notion of fellowship is witness. The new convert is not only to receive, he is to give. He is to witness, to tell others of the wonderful things God has done for him, and so fulfill the Lord's injunction to be a light in the midst of darkness. Witness is an important part of fellowship, and it is understood that a true convert is an apostle.

Nowhere does Graham suppose that conversion is a once-for-all event. Not only can this new life be lost, but it is capable of infinite degrees of development. He quotes II Corinthians (4:7) "We have this treasure in earthen vessels", and notes that we are not delivered completely yet, that our final completion will be in heaven.

Once converted we have to keep striving, even in spite of our falls, toward what John Wesley called "sanctification" or "perfect love". This, according to the Methodist Discipline, means that we are "not only delivered from the guilt of sin, but are saved from its power, and are enabled to love God with all our hearts and walk in His commandments blameless". This is a Spirit-filled life. Wesley described it as a life "fully surrendered".

This is the goal of the "born-again Christian". But Graham does not emphasize this "sanctification" or "perfect love" in his sermons and writings, and gives no indication whether he thinks many or few arrive at this goal.

To sum up. The elements of conversion are *repentance*, or a disgust and sorrow for and a turning away from our imperfect, divided, fragmented, and sinful lives; *faith* in, or acceptance of, with the whole person, mind, will and heart, Jesus Christ, who saves us and to whom we turn over our lives in total commitment; *rebirth* through the Holy Spirit, that is, a new life infused into the depths of our being, making for us all things new. This new life must be nurtured in us by faithful reading of the Scriptures, by prayer, and by active fellowship in the church.

5. Yes, But What About . . . ?

The last chapter gave a fairly complete picture of Graham's ideas on conversion, or decision for Christ. But it probably did not answer all the questions that leap to mind: What about emotionalism in the decision for Christ? What about free will and grace? Are we supposed to be overwhelmed by God's grace, or is the choice really a free one? What about instantaneous conversion? Does it happen in an instant, or is it gradual? What about Baptism, and joining a church, and so on? We turn now to these questions.

What about Emotionalism?

In the minds of most people pietism, or revivalism, or evangelicalism, is instinctively associated with grotesque and gaudy manifestations of what is claimed as "the Spirit". There is a long history of these "convulsions of piety", as William James terms them. The early Quakers, before becoming respectable and conducting their meetings "with order and decorum", were said, in a contemporary account, to "fall into dreadful Tremblings in their whole Bodies and Joints, with Risings and Swellings in their Bowels; Shriekings, Yellings, Howlings and Roarings". The French Prophets so called, or Camisards, indulged in "Shakings of their Heads, crawlings on their Knees, Quakings, Tremblings, Whistlings. . . . Howling in their Assemblies like a Dog". The Jansenist convulsionaries of Saint Médard did this sort of thing too, "swallowing pebbles, glass, and even live coals, women walking feet in air . . . groaning, singing, shrieking, whistling, declaiming, prophesying, caterwauling, etc., etc.". John Wesley details many manifestations like these which took place at his sermons; the entries in his Journal are frequent and cover a period of over 30 years, from 1755 to 1786. Jonathan Edwards, intellectual and theologian though he was, so aroused the emotions of his New England audiences that he had to ask them to restrain their groans and weeping so that he could continue preaching.

Charles Grandison Finney's congregation, he tells us, began to fall from their seats in every direction and cry for mercy. Another congregation were "some in kneeling posture, and some prostrate on the floor. Some bathing the temples of their friends with camphor, and rubbing them to keep them from fainting, and, so they feared, from dying". Revivalists have been known so to work up not only the crowd but themselves that they swooned away in the pulpit.

There is a long and not very edifying history of this sort of thing, from the ecstatic Montanists of the second century down to Elmer Gantry of yesterday and the snake handlers of North Carolina and some Pentecostals of today.

Billy Graham makes it crystal clear that he dissociates himself completely from this kind of Corybantic Christianity.

I have already mentioned my own surprise at the relative lack of emotion at a Graham crusade meeting. There is emotion present of course, but it is hushed, controlled, muted. Even though the meeting might be in a baseball stadium, the atmosphere is that of our middle-class, "respectable" churches. The music, though sentimental, is not charged with high emotion. It is in a lower key emotionally than 75% of our popular music in general and 90% of the style favored by our young people. Graham, perhaps conscious of some criticism in this matter, in recent years usually eliminates "Just As I Am, Without One Plea", formerly traditional at the invitation and in fact sung at his own conversion, as being too sentimental and emotional. During the sermon one does not hear any shouted "Amens" or "Hallelujahs" in reinforcement of the preacher's sentiments. Ushers are on hand to deal with such exuberance quietly but effectively. One is reminded of Billy Sunday's practice of telling such an enthusiast, "Two can't windjam at once, brother; let me do it".

This impression of the down-playing of emotion is corroborated by some of the conversion stories. A typical comment, from an English nurse, "I listened to Billy Graham as he preached, and I was quite surprised. I had expected to see something much more dramatic, but he was very conservative. The whole service was filled with a feeling of reverence".

In a sermon on this subject Graham clearly outlines the subordinate part of emotion in the process of conversion. The title is, significantly, "Facts, Faith and Feeling". The facts precede the faith, for our belief is not merely subjective; it has an objective basis in the historical facts of the Gospel event. Trusting in Christ is trusting not in a figment of someone's imagination, but in fact. The faith we have is an experience, but it is not necessarily a highly emotional experience.

Feeling is the last of the three words, and it must remain last in your thinking. I believe that earnest and honest seekers for the salvation of God have unrest and uncertainty when they determine that they must have some kind of state of emotion to make conversion an experience in their lives . . .

I have read carefully through the New Testament to see just what kind of experience you are entitled to. I have looked to see what the nature of the experience of conversion is, and have found that the New Testament sets forth only one. There is one experience for which you can look, and that is the experience of faith.

Believing is an experience as real as any experience, yet multitudes are looking for something more—some electric sensation that will bring a thrill to their physical bodies, or some other spectacular manifestation. Many have been told to look for such spiritual thrills, but the Bible says that "a man is justified by faith", and not by feeling. A man is saved by trusting in the finished work of Christ on the cross and not by bodily sensations and religious ecstasy . . .

Certainly there is room for feeling in saving faith, but we are not saved by it. Whatever feeling there may be is the *result* of saving faith, but feeling never saved a single soul.

Then he goes on to explain that, as a result of faith, and of understanding just what Christ has done for me, I naturally respond with gratitude and love. And I develop confidence, and joy, and inward peace, and so on. These are all feelings. They are not however of the essence of faith; they are a result of it.

"Too many people", he says elsewhere, "make the mistake of measuring the intensity of their salvation by their feelings. Don't make this serious mistake. Take Him at His word". Faith then is a leap in the dark, sometimes, very often in fact, without the warmth and glow of emotional support.

This preeminence of faith as an assent to something objective over faith as an emotion is underlined by Dr. Robert Ferm, a prominent member of the Graham organization, in his book on the psychology of conversion:

The uniqueness of the evangelical crisis lies, not in the psychological symptoms, but in the object about which the Christian personality is integrated . . . The emphasis will be upon what is believed, rather than upon the activity of believing, or even upon one of the many possible emotions which constitute the emphasis of mysticism in its various forms. The way to God is by submission to objective fact, not by the route suggested in the words of Bernard of Clairvaux, previously quoted: "The road to God is through the affections, not the intellect; we come to know God by love rather than learning". The objection to what is implied in this statement is that love depends upon an enlightened mind. The words of the Scripture (*Romans* 5:8) "God commendeth his love toward us, in that, while we were yet sinners, Christ died for us", indicate specific knowledge issuing in love. No unenlightened emotion may impart salvation to the soul.

The evangelical crisis is one that is brought about by faith in specific truth redemptive in its character.

Without saying anything else about this statement, let us make this one comment: if one were expecting some defense of emotion from someone as high in the Graham inner circle as Dr. Ferm is, in a book with an approving introduction by Billy Graham himself, this is a surprising statement. But there it is, and it is in the context of his contention that the uniqueness of the Christian or evangelical conversion, as distinguished from every other kind, is that it is centered on the objective reality of the person of Jesus Christ.

Graham himself is hardheaded when assessing the lasting value of conversions made under emotion. Good works are the sure sign of real conversion. The good tree brings forth good fruit. "There are thousands of people who have had some form of emotional experience that they refer to as conversion but who have never been truly converted to Christ. Christ demands a change in the way you live—but if your life does not conform to your experience, then you have every reason to doubt your experience".

Given what has just been said, the reader can judge for himself the validity of the following comment by a prominent Catholic theologian: "Billy Graham's 'crusade' is like the older revivals. It is an excitation of emotion as a self-justifying act. Graham has dropped out the more obvious defects palpable in men like Billy Sunday. There are now no cheap theatrics. There is no emotionalism, i.e., calculated arousing of uncontrolled feeling. There is no militant anti-intellectualism. But there is still the relegation of the intellect to the realm of the irrelevant. The search is not for the truth, but only for the felt good".

I have stressed this point, perhaps overly, but only to counterbalance any *a priori* impression that Graham, as an evangelical pietist, must naturally be quite emotional. ("Isn't emotion the stock-in-trade of an evangelical?") In so doing we have to guard against giving the opposite impression that emotion plays no part, or an insignificant part, in Graham's preaching or in his conversions.

He is careful not to underestimate the role of the emotions. He says we have leaned over too far in the church to avoid the charge of emotionalism. In contemporary society we see nothing incongruous in giving vent to our emotions in sports, in entertainment, radio, politics, the theater. We expose our feelings to others, to the psychiatrist, even to the public, in almost every phase of our lives—except in religion. "I think we have de-emphasized emotionalism too much; and I think we have emphasized intellectualism too much". Men still need to be moved toward God. Scripture is full of examples of this: Moses, Isaiah, David, Mary Magdalene, the disciples at Emmaus, with their hearts burning within them. He quotes an English sermon: "What is wrong with emotion? Christianity is falling in love with Christ. Has anyone ever fallen in love without emotion? Can we imagine somebody advising a young lover by saying, 'I would not marry her if I were you—you evidently feel deeply about it'. How could anyone come into contact with the living Christ and feel both His forgiving love and His relentless challenge and not have deep emotion?"

Then Graham continues: "No, you cannot be converted to Jesus Christ through an emotional experience alone; but emotion has its place. The church today has been so anxious to be intellectually respectable and to have perfect decorum and dignity that the reality, joy and thrill of Christian experience have been overlooked and sometimes forgotten. Christ is a real, living Person who can transform the life until men not only *think* but also *feel*".

In summary then, to the question, what is the role of the emotions in conversion, Graham answers: a subordinate and supporting role, but an important one nonetheless.

What about Grace and Free Will?

Graham emphasizes free will a great deal in conversion by insisting on the importance of decision. Especially in the crusades is this evident. Everything in the meetings is designed to lead up to the moment of the invitation, when Graham solicits a here-and-now decision for Christ. The audience is asked to make a definite act of will, to do something, to come forward. He asks them "to come", "come out of your seats", "get up and come". They are also asked to sign a decision card, which concretizes and specifies this act of will.

A similar emphasis is observed by examining his radio sermons. Out of a random sampling of 36 sermons, 28 were found to have a specific, pointed appeal for an act of will. Almost every one of these appeals was made at the conclusion of the sermon, in fact, in the very last sentence. Note the concluding words of these sermons: "Will you open your heart to Jesus Christ right now?" And, ". . . so it all boils down to you. You have to accept Christ. You have to become a Christian. You have to say yes to Christ. And right now where you sit or stand or ride, wherever you are. You can say a simple yes to Christ. Make your decision for Him, live for Him, and it is America through you making its decision". Again, "You can settle this matter between you and God right now. You can get right with God by receiving Christ as your personal Savior. Let him come into your heart".

The emphasis is not only on a personal act of will, but also on an immediate act of will—today, at this moment, right now, wherever you are. "You will never find it easier to accept Christ than at this moment. To delay one moment is to find it harder. 'Now is the accepted time', says the Bible, 'now is the day of salvation'. It is a delusion to think that tomorrow will be better than today. Faith in tomorrow rather than faith in Christ is a delusion that will cause you to be finally and eternally lost".

There is an urgency, a now-or-never-ness about this appeal which dramatizes the situation and highlights the importance of *decision.* It would seem that salvation depends upon decision, decision now, and decision exclusively.

Erroll Hulse, by no means a friendly critic, puts the matter somewhat in caricature but I believe with substantial accuracy, when he writes: "The will, urges the preacher, is free, free to break with the Devil, free to lay hold upon the hope set before it, free to allow the Lord to make good His sovereign rights and claims, or free to reject the overtures of grace, free to turn from God to the Devil, free to choose perdition rather than good, free to believe to the saving of the soul. Eternity hangs on the decision of the human will in this fateful moment or moments. The creature must decide."

Hulse reproves Graham for departing from the classic and original doctrine of the reformers by thus emphasizing free will. In his judgment of Graham's position, of course, Hulse is quite correct. Graham explicitly parts company with Calvinism by repudiating the concept of irresistible grace, and by implication the doctrines of predestination in the Calvinistic sense and limited atonement. In this he is following the tradition of American revivalistic thought after the time of the Calvinist Jonathan Edwards.

A good example of this outlook is Charles Grandison Finney, as illustrated in his noted sermon on the "New Heart", which was attacked vigorously by the heresy hunters among the conservative Calvinists of his time. Preaching on Ezekiel 18:31, "Make you a new heart and a new spirit, for why will ye die?" Finney asks why God should give us a command if he knows we have no power to obey. Since then God requires men to make themselves a new heart on pain of eternal death, it follows that men are able to do it. By emphasizing the part a man played in his own conversion, Finney neglected the supernatural. He made only a slight obeisance to the agency of the Holy Spirit, and concentrated on the human factors in conversion, i.e., the right use of means on the part of the preacher and a firm, resolute decision on the part of the convert.

Graham is not guilty of this. Time and time again he insists on the Holy Spirit as the principal agent in conversion. "I don't think I ever lead anybody to Christ. It is the Holy Spirit," he says. He puts great reliance on supernatural means in conversion, especially prayer. In speaking of the preparations for the New York crusade he lays great stress on the all-night prayer groups in Formosa, on the 400 people in prayer every morning at sunrise in Naga, India, on the other groups all over the world, even in Red China, Poland, Yugoslavia, 109 countries in all, interceding for the outpouring of God's grace on the New York crusade.

"We must always remember", he says, "that the Holy Spirit is the communicating agent. Without the Holy Spirit there would be no such thing as conversion". And again, "Thus the Bible teaches that man can undergo a radical spiritual and moral change that is brought about by God Himself. The word that Jesus used, and which is translated 'again' actually means 'from above'. The context of the third chapter of John teaches that the new birth is something that God does for man when man is willing to yield to God. As we have already seen, the Bible teaches that man is dead in trespasses and sins, and his great need is *life*".

As we have seen, for Graham there are three elements in conversion, repentance and faith, which he says are man's part, and rebirth, which he says is God's part. But even the part he attributes to man cannot be effected without the intervention of God. This is evident on a close examination of text and context, even in the many sermons in which he sounds like a semi-Pelagian. That is, in these sermons he sounds as though man makes some initial steps in God's direction on his own, without God's help, and then God intervenes and takes man the rest of the way. Thus, "When we are willing to turn from sin, then God will help us". Christ will not forgive sins until we turn. The moment we turn, we are forgiven. In some sermons he seems to say that we make some move, on our own, in God's direction, and then the next move is God's.

But a closer reading of the material would seem to absolve Graham of the charge of semi-Pelagianism, although he is sometimes less than accurate in expression. This is understandable, since he is not writing a treatise of theology, but preaching a sermon, and it should be noted, a sermon of exhortation to cooperate with God's grace. In this kind of exhortation he would naturally emphasize cooperation rather than the grace of God.

Elsewhere he makes it clear that even the first steps in the process are God's. Thus, even in the part he attributes to man, repentance for example, he says that the Holy Spirit makes us realize that we are sinners and directs our faith. Human nature in its unredeemed state is helpless to think good thoughts, to do good deeds, to measure up to God's requirements. The cross tells the earnest seeker and the anxious inquirer that by their efforts they are not made one whit better. Repentance involves conviction, and this means that the Holy Spirit acts on our dead souls. "But you say, 'I will resolve to do better. I will muster all my will power, and revise my way of living'. That is noble, but futile. A corpse could as well say, 'I will through sheer effort rise out of the coffin and be a living man again' ".

In speaking of man's part in conversion by the use of his free will, he usually speaks in terms of an activity which is not initial; it is usually described as a response to a stimulus, a reaction to an action. Thus God is usually represented as giving an invitation and man responding. On man's part then willing takes the form of accepting Christ, receiving Christ. A man can't earn or purchase salvation, he can only take it. One of Graham's favorite texts is that from St. John's prologue, "But to all who did accept him, he gave power to become children of God".

Graham often uses the words *surrender* and *commit*, and commit he explains, means to let go, to relinquish, to abandon yourself to Christ.

William James also speaks of this surrender in conversion as passivity rather than activity, as relaxation, letting go, resigning, giving up responsibility. Thus described, it seems almost nonvoluntary, an abstention from decision, like someone in a meeting not voting either yes or no, but simply abstaining. In the last analysis of course, it is an act of will, but a different kind of will act. C.S. Lewis in his *Surprised by Joy* speaks of his own conversion as a giving in. "I gave in, and admitted that God was God, and knelt and prayed: perhaps, that night, the most dejected and reluctant convert in all England. . . . I say 'I chose', yet it did not really seem possible to do the opposite. . . .

You could argue that I was not a free agent, but I am
more inclined to think that this came nearer to being a
perfectly free act than most that I have ever done. Ne-
cessity may not be the opposite of freedom, and perhaps a man is most free when instead of producing motives, he could only say, 'I am what I do' ".

To sum up: Graham is no Calvinist—man has free
will and contributes something to his conversion and
salvation; but he is no Pelagian either—man cannot
save himself; he needs God's grace from the very beginning of the conversion process.

As for the theological problem involved in all this,
the tension between God's sovereign grace and man's
free will, he says, "There is a mystery in one aspect of
conversion that I have never been able to fathom and I
have never read a book of theology that satisfied me at
this point—the relationship between the sovereignty of
God and man's free will. It seems to me that they are
both taught in the Scriptures and both are involved.
Certainly we are taught to proclaim the kerygma and
man is besought to respond by repentance and faith".

In noting that both the sovereignty of God and
man's free will are clearly taught in Scripture and then
consigning the reconciling of these two to the realm of
mystery, Graham is on safe and traditional, and sensi-
ble, ground.

What about Instantaneous Conversion?

Conversion in the evangelical tradition is a definite, notable, memorable event, with a clear-cut before
and after. The convert is delivered from his old life so
definitively that he seems to himself a new person be-

ginning a new existence. The "rebirth" is a happening, an event, which can be dated and even pinpointed as definitely as the date of his natural birth.

Thus Wesley tells of 652 members of his Society in London who all testified that their deliverance from sin was instantaneous, wrought in a moment. Hence he concludes that conversion is "commonly, if not always, an instantaneous work". A good example of this is the conversion in Rome in 1842 of Alphonse Ratisbonne, a free-thinking French Jew. Before his remarkable change in the church of St. Andrea delle Fratte he was irreligious, even antipathetic to Catholicism. After his change he seems a completely new person, becomes a priest, a Jesuit, a founder of two religious congregations.

Not many conversions involve such a dramatic about-face, though in the evangelical tradition conversion involves *per se* a change that is remarkable and notable. In the abundant literature of conversion, case after case is cited where a radically new direction is taken. The indifferent become devotees, drunkards turn sober, drifters become responsible, lechers pure, scoffers believe, the fearful become confident, the aimless purposeful, the cynical unworldly, the proud humble. And all this at a definite point of time.

This is the pure type, what the literature of evangelical conversion calls the definite crisis type. There is a quite definable crisis, a decisive moment. The analogy is from medicine, where crisis is that change in the progress of a disease which indicates whether the result is to be recovery or death. Here the result is a definite change of direction, of attitude, of purpose. This change in most cases can be clearly recalled and situated in time. It does not have to be absolutely instantaneous, but only relatively so, over a period of a day or two. Nor must it be instantaneous in the sense of being without ascertainable preparation, as in the case of St. Paul. Most cases of crisis conversion have varying degrees of preparation up till the decisive moment; witness St. Augustine. Even Ratisbonne, a few days before his remarkable conversion, hung a medal of the Blessed Virgin around his neck and read a short prayer to the Virgin, half in jest, to please a Catholic friend who was trying to convert him.

Of the 36 converts from the Graham crusades whose histories are given in Robert Ferm's *Persuaded to Live*, almost all had some kind of preparation or build-up before the decisive moment: some vague notion of Christianity, or perhaps some haphazard religious upbringing, or some intermittent attendance at church or Sunday school. A few were even externally active in Sunday school teaching or other church activity. Many had a problem: alcohol, disappointment in love, or conscious unhappiness, unease, restlessness, a felt need that prepared the way for what followed—the resolution of the crisis, and consequent relief.

What does Billy Graham himself say in this matter? He writes: "We may say, therefore, that conversion can be an instantaneous event, a crisis in which the person receives a clear revelation of the love of God; or it can be a gradual unfolding accompanied by a climactic moment at the time the line is crossed between darkness and light, between death and life everlasting. But it may not happen in either of these ways. My wife, for example, cannot remember the exact day or hour when she became a Christian, but she is certain that there was such a moment in her life, a moment when she actually crossed the line. Many young people who have

grown up in Christian homes and had the benefit of
Christian training are unaware of the time when they
committed their lives to Christ".

Graham's three-fold division should be compared
with E.T. Clark's division into (1) definite crisis type,
(2) emotional stimulus type, and (3) gradual awakening
type. The definite crisis type has been explained above.
The emotional stimulus type can be described thus:
there is no upheaval, no special change is effected, but
the subject looks back on some event which served as a
stimulus to awaken his religious consciousness. Life
and attitude remain unchanged, but the stimulus stands
out in memory as the dawn of a definite religious acceptance. The emotional stimulus type is thus distinguished from the crisis type in that it involves no radical change of orientation, but a reinforcement of the
orientation already present; it differs on the other hand
from the gradual awakening type in that it involves a
memory of some definite stimulus as the start of a
clear-cut and whole-hearted acceptance instead of only
formalistic or perfunctory adhesion.

The third type, gradual awakening, without either
a crisis or an emotional stimulus to fix the moment of
conversion, or of some kind of definite change, is an
anomaly to an evangelical. Yet Graham has to face the
fact: "I find many Christians who have grown up in
Christian homes, been baptized or confirmed and had
the benefit of Christian training, who are unaware of
the time when they committed their lives to Christ, yet
their faith and lives clearly testify that they know
Christ".

Graham explains that those who are converted,
even though they can't remember when, are certain that
they have crossed the line. He even speaks of people

being converted to Christ, "consciously or unconsciously". This is surely conversion in a nonevangelical
sense. The evangelical knows when he is converted; he
cannot be converted unconsciously. It is an event, not a
gradual process.

Here we have two entirely different concepts of
Christian life. One stresses Christian education and
nurture, a constant attention to the tender plant, a careful bringing along, an *educatio*, in the sense of leading
or bringing out the already existing Christian life into
the full flowering of all its potential. This presupposes
that the Christian life has already been bestowed by
Baptism in a rudimentary but essential way. Attention
is paid to the organic and gradual growth of a planting
that has been made early, very often, and even usually,
without the subject's consciousness. The aim of this education is to make the young Christian conscious of his
real situation so that he responds with awareness to the
objective salvation he has without any personal merit
received.

The other concept is that salvation *initially* not
merely *later* has to come through conscious participation and acceptance of the gift of God. A person must
experience in his conscious life that he is saved, to commit himself knowingly and willingly through faith to
Jesus Christ as his Savior and Lord. As we noted, Graham discounts the need for deep emotion in this commitment. It may be a commitment in sheer, naked,
trusting faith, with little emotional resonance, in a kind
of rudimentary dark night of the soul. But knowing and
willing it must be, otherwise no salvation occurs. Thus
it has a definitiveness, an identifiable moment, which
makes it a kind of watershed of one's life.

Graham, not following the strictly evangelical line,

admits both kinds of conversion. He broadens his concept of conversion to include even Christian nurture or
"the nurture of grace" as he calls it, as long as it issues
in some conscious religious experience, some vital con-
frontation with Christ.

The question I want to raise is this; is the theology of
adult conversion fundamentally different from that of a
child who is cradled in the faith and nurtured in the arms
of the Church? It is my opinion that we ought not to
contrast the "nurture of grace" and the "grace of conversion" as many have tried to do. I am convinced that
there are both, and happy is the man who by the nurture of grace is brought to the grace of conversion.
Conversion can be an ultimate and proper fulfillment of
all that baptism meant to the child, and perhaps later
even in confirmation. Conversion must express itself in
life as a change of mind, a radical break with the past,
and a total commitment to Christ for the future.
Whether conversion happens suddenly in adulthood or
gradually through childhood is beside the point. The
thing that counts is that it happens.

And in another place, in answer to a question:

I don't say that it is a once for all experience. I say that
when a person comes to Christ—let's say in one of our
crusades—that this is the first step in his life toward the
Kingdom of God, or it may be his second step, but it is
a step. Christ said it is like birth. There is the moment
of conception, then there are nine months of gestation,
then the actual birth. When a person comes under the
sound of the Gospel, whether it be in a local church, or
in an individual contact or whatever, it may be a moment of conception or it may be another step in gestation, or it may be an actual birth. And then they go on
to growth in Christ.

Is conversion then in Graham's thought instantaneous or gradual? In most cases and ideally, instantaneous, even though often with a certain previous preparation or build-up to the decisive moment. In many other cases, which however remain the minority, the conversion may be gradual, even imperceptible.

What about the Church? What about Baptism?

As for Baptism, it may be surprising, but Graham practically never mentions Baptism as something to be undergone by the convert in the process of conversion. In a rare reference to Baptism he quotes Mahatma Gandhi as saying: "If a man really has found God through discovering Jesus Christ, then he must be baptized and show the world that he is a follower of Jesus, else he will be a living lie". Gandhi of course had studied the New Testament, knew that Baptism was the Christian rite of initiation and took it for granted that if one were converted to Christianity he would be baptized. But Graham almost never even mentions Baptism. One might wonder why.

This is not an easy question to answer. Graham was baptized by sprinkling when he joined the Presbyterian church as a boy. Later, as a student at Florida Bible Institute, he became involved in revival preaching in a number of Baptist churches, and was so successful that he was offered a Baptist pulpit on a regular basis. The only difficulty, Graham replied, was that he was a Presbyterian. He was asked if he would become a Baptist and consent to Baptism by immersion. He asked to pray about it, telephoned his parents to get their approval, got it, and was baptized in Silver Lake near Palatka, Florida, on December 4, 1938, just 20 years old. During the following year he was ordained by the ministerial association at Peniel, Florida. At present he is a member of the Southern Baptist Church of Dallas, one of the biggest, if not the biggest Baptist congregation in the world. In spite of living away from Dallas and spending much time traveling, he makes it a point to preach once or twice a year in the Dallas church, and faithfully tithes to support that church.

Graham does not take a "high" sacramental view of Baptism. For a Southern Baptist, the sacrament is a public profession of faith in Jesus Christ. It is a sign of regeneration and the other consequent effects. But it is not an efficacious sign. It does not effect that which it signifies. This is done extra-sacramentally by the person's accepting Christ in repentance and faith and by the Holy Spirit's action in regeneration. Baptism should be accepted because Christ commanded it, but for no other reason.

Another point to be borne in mind: Graham does not mention Baptism as a step in conversion in the United States because there he is preaching to audiences many of whom, if not most, are already baptized. About 60% of the people in the United States in 1957 had some form of Christian church membership, and according to a survey made in 1965 92% had some "Christian preference". Holding as he does that the sacrament is merely a sign, he is not anxious about rebaptism because of fear of possible invalidity in a previous Baptism. Further, he urges that the convert or inquirer join a church "where Christ is preached". These are for the most part churches that insist on Baptism: if the person has not been baptized, he will be on entrance to this church. Thus, Graham's preaching in effect often results in the reception of Baptism.

In this way, he avoids the controversial question of infant Baptism and the connected question of rebaptism of those who were baptized as infants, sometimes burning issues among Protestants. Rather than enter into theological controversy on these points, Graham limits himself strictly to preaching conversion to Christ in the sense of accepting him in faith and repentance. From there the convert will go to a Christian church. In the church it will be determined that he was either previously baptized or not. If he was not, he will be baptized. If he was, then his previous Baptism will either be recognized, or he will be rebaptized. In all three situations, the person either becomes or is baptized.

It may be objected that this silence, this indirection, not emphasizing something which Scripture does emphasize, which was very important to the early church, is making light of Baptism.

It is hard to ignore the communal aspect of conversion in the New Testament. The call is not only to Jesus Christ but to a community gathered around him. Salvation is presented in the Synoptics time and time again as entrance into a kingdom, the kingdom of God or the kingdom of heaven. There is in the Christians of the New Testament a vivid awareness of their collective identity as the *qahal* or religious assembly of the new Israel. In the early chapters of Acts the believers are represented as a very closely knit body, united heart and soul, having everything in common (5:32), taking care of their own poor, even by a separate order of deacons created especially for this purpose (c. 6). In the early church, acceptance of Christ as Lord and Savior meant acceptance of the brotherhood and the brotherhood's acceptance of the convert into the common life, the *koinonia*. To accept Christ as Savior and to join the church, the *ekklesia*, were synonymous. It would be unthinkable for a man in apostolic times to become a Christian and to go his own way with little contact with the church.

In this context the rite of initiation was of prime importance. The apostolic community was formed in the double act of prophetic proclamation and baptizing. In Baptism the action was that of incorporation into the messianic kingdom. By this act the new Christian was made a member of the new Israel of God, of a holy nation, a chosen people, an inheritor of the promises. Baptism is an assignment to Christ, a dedication to Christ, an incorporation into Christ. It is the salvation event, that by which we are saved. For St. Paul it is the ontological act of being taken into Christ's death and resurrection and so sharing, being caught up with him, in his death and resurrection, and thus saved. It was the very essence of conversion, of the passage from death to life.

Graham's omission of Baptism from his preaching, it seems to me, can only be explained by saying that he is not preaching the whole Christian message, only what he considers the essential message. He is an evangelist, not a teacher. He is limiting himself to announcing salvation, and then letting the churches spell out in detail the means of salvation. By thus limiting his function quite narrowly to that of announcing salvation, without stressing this means of Baptism, Graham (although he had not read Finney when he began this practice) is essentially following Finney's advice, noted above: "The true Philosophy of promoting and consummating an excitement and publick action upon any subject is to confine the publick mind to *a point.* . . . Revivals of religion afford almost endless illustration of this. Introduce Baptism, Election, or any other doctrine that does not bear on the question of immediate acceptance of Christ and you either Kill or retard the work".

This consideration, together with the one noted above, that in any case the converts either will be already baptized or become baptized on becoming active in a church, can, I think, explain Graham's policy in this matter.

As for Graham's thinking on the church, the first thing to be made clear is that he is not starting a separate or new church. In this he is being true to the pietistic tradition. The man who is regarded as the father of Pietism, Philipp Jakob Spener, had no idea of starting a church. His aim rather was to leaven the Lutheran mass by rallying within it small devotional circles which would obey the neglected call of piety, "ecclesiolae in ecclesia", devoted to intensive Bible study and a fervent spiritual life. Count Zinzendorf likewise wanted his Moravian brethren at Herrnhut to remain within Lutheranism and exercise the same function, as a kind of religious order within the parent body. John Wesley did not wish to establish Methodism as a separate denomination—his Societies were not a church—but rather to infuse a new spirit of fervent piety into the Church of England. He lived and died a member of that church, and it was only after his death that his followers seceded.

Ronald Knox says of Moravianism that it is "essentially neither a doctrine nor a discipline, but a spirituality. And that spirituality owes nothing to the Middle Ages; it is German Pietism refracted through the curious lens of Zinzendorf's own speculation. Like Jansenism, like Wesleyanism, it is in part a reaction against the Deistic thought of the day, which offered to

the human soul a barren nourishment of Christianity
without Christ".

This has certain applications to our present situation. What Graham is doing is not inculcating any new
doctrine or discipline beyond what is "traditionally
Christian". He is preaching a spirituality that is Chris-
tocentric, "experimental", fervent, warm, a spirit of encounter with Christ as one's personal Savior, in the
midst of a clerical establishment which often, if not
quite offering the human soul "a barren nourishment of
Christianity without Christ", often at least dilutes the
diet.

But what is Graham's thought on the church itself?
One has the impression in reading his sermons and articles that the church does not play a very important
part in his thinking. True, he asks his converts or inquirers to join a church, but the impression is given that
this is purely for them, for their own interest, not for
the church. The church is almost merely a means to
safeguard their new-found life gained through the rebirth. The emphasis is on what has been called "me and
Jesus" spirituality. True, he asks his new converts to
"witness" to let others know of what they have found in
Christ. That is, to promote encounters of the same kind
in other people, to propagate the "me and Jesus" spirituality. This is not said in condemnation. I am merely
pointing out that the aim seems to be to promote what
is, in today's jargon, the vertical relationship. The hori-
zontal relationship, between Christian and Christian, is
not stressed, at least as an integral constituent of the
Christian life. There is little emphasis on salvation in
and through the church, on the church as a mediator of
salvation, little or nothing of God's will to save men
through community, in a Mystical Body, no hint of the

church as the new Israel of God, as the People of God.

In an article written for *The Christian Century* however he seems to give the lie to these statements:

A fourth change is to be seen in the fact that during the past ten years my concept of the church has taken on greater dimension. Ten years ago my concept of the church tended to be narrow and provincial, but after a decade of intimate contact with Christians the world over I am now aware that the family of God contains people of various theological, cultural, class and denominational differences. I have learned that there can even be minor disagreements of theology, methods and motives but that within the true church there is a mysterious unity that overrides all divisive factors.

In groups which in my ignorant piousness I formerly "frowned upon" I have found men so dedicated to Christ and so in love with the truth that I have felt unworthy to be in their presence. I have learned that although Christians do not always agree, they can disagree agreeably, and that what is most needed in the church today is for us to show an unbelieving world that we love one another.

To me the church has become a great, glorious and triumphant organism. It is the body of Christ, and the humblest member is an important part of that body. I have also come to believe that within every visible church there is a group of regenerated, dedicated disciples of Christ.

The title of this is "What Ten Years Have Taught Me". It is an article, not a sermon. His ideas on the church are developing and broadening, but they are still susceptible to much further development, and they have not shown up in a significant, sustained way in his sermons since that article was written, in 1960. In fact quite recently, in 1969, preaching to young people and sympathizing with their evaluation of the institutional church, he says:

And that's the trouble with young people today. They're waiting for a hand-me-down religion, and they have discarded Christianity because they say, "It hasn't worked in my parents' lives; my parents are big hypocrites. It didn't work for them".

You see, you have a caricature of Christianity. I'm not really asking you to come to Christianity as an institution. I'm asking you to have a personal relationship with Jesus Christ on your own—your own experience.

As can be seen from the above and from other writings, he has a broad notion of the church as embracing all who believe in Christ and are united in some sort of visible fellowship, without worrying about questions of doctrine (beyond "traditional orthodoxy" as explained above), worship or church order. In other words, all churches, or ecclesial communities in the terminology of Vatican II (*Lumen Gentium*), which owe their allegiance in some way to Jesus Christ, are church, are part of the People of God. This approach enables Graham to win the cooperation of ministerial associations across a very broad theological spectrum, and thus have access to a much wider audience than he would if he had a more specific notion of the church. Here again, he is applying Finney's pragmatism, not introducing into his preaching "any other doctrine that does not bear on the question of the immediate acceptance of Christ".

To sum up, Graham's doctrine on Baptism and the church is undeveloped, or, perhaps more accurately, unstressed, for the reason that these considerations are in his mind, in relation to the definite and limited aim to which he has set himself, secondary.

6. The Critics

Billy Graham's critics are legion. Their criticisms range from the trivial—"I don't like his Southern accent"—to the basic—"He's preaching a false Christianity". The tone varies from the condescending tolerance of J.B. Priestley—"I did not find him personally disagreeable"—to the outraged indignation of Dr. Bob Jones, Jr.—"Billy Graham is a false teacher who is doing more harm to the cause of Christ than any living man". His fundamentalist critics say he has sold out to the modernists; these same "modernists" (although they would not be happy with that designation) say he is preaching an oversimplified, old-fashioned Christianity that they do not find credible. Others, from various points of view, attack the theology underlying Graham's revivals, his emphasis on decision and free will, his neglect of the social gospel, his reducing religion to something too simple and/or too easy. Still others concentrate their criticisms on his evangelistic methods: too much organization, they say, or too much psychological manipulation. Yet others hammer away at the quality of results, claiming that a large proportion of the "conversions" do not last.

There are so many critics that it is difficult to do them all justice within the confines of this chapter. Our method will be to deal with their criticisms, rather than individual critics, except incidentally, since over the past 20 years the same criticisms have been repeated many times by different critics. We shall examine the *pattern* of criticism.

Excluded from consideration here will be two

kinds of criticisms, (1) the superficial ones: judgments about Graham's accent, taste in clothes, voice, smile, etc., (2) those which take us out of the field of his proper work and into the realm of personal preference: his attitude toward the labor unions, toward the universities, or toward the world political situation.

In examining the multiplicity of these criticisms we find they fall pretty much into two categories: theological and methodological, that is, criticisms of his theology, and criticisms of his procedure in the crusades. These categories sometimes overlap: his procedures have theological implications, and his theology results in specific procedures. However, the division, though somewhat arbitrary, is a convenient one, and we shall proceed with it.

I
CRITICISMS OF GRAHAM'S THEOLOGY

*Does Graham Place Excessive Emphasis
on Decision and Freedom of Will?*

Erroll Hulse, in his book, *Billy Graham—The Pastor's Dilemma*, hits Graham's emphasis on "decision" very hard. Graham, for him, is departing from the "whole counsel of God", which for Hulse means Luther's and Calvin's concept of man's inability to do anything about his own salvation. Those Reformers believed man's will is so vitiated by the fall that it either has no freedom of choice at all (Calvin) or at least in the matter of salvation has no freedom (Luther). This of course is not the Catholic doctrine that man's will of itself is insufficient for man's salvation. This position involves the classic doctrines of unconditional election, limited atonement and irresistible grace. This for Hulse, is "the whole counsel of God", which is not declared by Graham, who very definitely insists that a person has a part in his own salvation, by asking that a person make a choice, and make it now.

We have already seen that Graham does indeed hold freedom of will, but on the other hand holds that the human will is incapable of making salutary acts without God's grace, even from the beginning of the conversion process, and so is neither Pelagian nor semi-Pelagian. When Hulse says that Graham has departed from the original doctrine of the Reformation in the matter of free will, he is perfectly correct. But many, if not most, contemporary Protestant theologians have done the same thing.

Hulse is on firmer ground when he criticizes Graham not only for his emphasis on decision, but for his emphasis on decision *now*, his call for *immediate* decision. "The repetitive manner in which every meeting *must* conclude with a call for *immediate* response, is itself an eloquent confession of credence in the natural ability of man . . . an integral part of the preaching is the 'call for decisions' with the full expectancy that in the logical sequence of cause and effect, results must accrue".

It must be admitted that Graham's insistence on an immediate, here-and-now response is a constant feature of his appeal. "Today", "right now", "wherever you are", are constantly recurring expressions in his appeals for decision. This is certainly a useful device for soliciting the cooperation of man's free will with the grace of God. But it also poses a difficulty.

Let us admit that on the one hand man's will is

free, and on the other that it cannot act without the grace of God. It cannot act unless helped to act. But who knows when that moment is? Graham says typically in his sermons, "This is the moment, and this is the hour". . . "If you're ever to come, it's now". . ."This is your night". "To delay one moment is to find it harder . . . It is a delusion to think that tomorrow will be better than today. Faith in tomorrow rather than faith in Christ is a delusion that will cause you to be finally and eternally lost".

It is true that Graham insists that a man can only come to Christ when the Spirit of God is drawing him. Yet on the other hand he insists time and time again that people come to Christ tonight, now, this moment. This can only mean that for Graham the Spirit of God is drawing people tonight, now, this moment. How does he know this? There is no way of knowing with certainty. Of course, one might argue to this from the fact that God wants to save all, and from the fact that many concurrent circumstances are coming together in this crusade meeting: the preaching of the Word of God, the need of the individual souls for Christ, the splendid opportunity that is before them to accept Christ at this time, the prayers of so many Christians to this end for them. If there ever were a time of grace, is not this the time? Can you imagine a better time? If in the life of every adult there comes some time for making a decision that will save or damn, a moment of choosing God and Christ or self, good or evil, is not this the time? All this argues with some cogency that the grace of God is almost certainly moving some and probably moving many in the audience to accept Christ at the moment of the invitation.

But it is also true that we have no certain way of

knowing how many are thus being moved. Graham acts as if *all* were being moved: "Get up now and come. You come. Your family and friends will wait for you. This is your hour. I want you to come out of your seats, by the hundreds. . . . Just get up and come". There is in all this the danger of running ahead of the grace of God, of hastening conversion, or hurrying some souls into an on-the-spot, premature decision.

Good spiritual direction respects the initiative of the Spirit, who breathes where he wills. No man can command the Spirit, even in a good cause; he can only pray for his coming, and be docile to his movements. Nor can a man command an action (decision) that depends on the Spirit as though the Spirit were available on demand. "God is not like an automatic slot machine that responds when the coin drops into the box, nor is he like an electric current available to the man who will just plug in".

This is the danger of authoritatively, or even persuadingly, telling *all* without distinction to accept Christ here and now. Is there then no place for a general invitation? Yes there is, if it is addressed, as it sometimes but rarely is, in conditional or provisional terms. Something like the following might be said: "God is surely speaking to many of you tonight. Each one should ask himself, isn't this message meant for *me* . . . if it is, then you get up and come . . ."

This is of course a makeshift. The ideal way would be for a skilled spiritual director to judge the state of the person's dispositions and guide him accordingly. Graham himself has done this in individual cases, putting off the conversion of someone he knows isn't ready. This of course cannot be done while preaching to 50,000 people. It is one of the unavoidable limitations of a crusade—which may be partially, but only partially, compensated for by the gesture in the direction of the Holy Spirit suggested above, and by a vastly improved system of spiritual counseling.

It may be objected that the biblical accounts of conversion emphasize the suddenness of conversion, without any spiritual direction, like the case of the 3,000 Christians baptized on the day of Pentecost, the Philippian jailer, the Ethiopian eunuch, Cornelius, and others. But these were unusual cases and were accompanied by a remarkable outpouring of the Spirit so manifest that no one could doubt it. This is not the case in a Graham crusade. The more typical situation of New Testament preaching and conversion is portrayed elsewhere in Acts, where Paul, and whoever is with him, Barnabas, Silas, Luke, will come into a city, start preaching and remain there for some time, as long as results are forthcoming. In Corinth it is 18 months, in Antioch over a year, in Ephesus two years, in the Roman captivity two whole years, all the whole "preaching and teaching" (*Acts* 28:31) all who came to them. This normal pattern of Paul's preaching implies personal and individual direction.

The problem of hurrying conversion has another aspect. Sound spiritual direction respects not only the initiative of the Spirit, but the laws of nature and in particular of natural organic growth. Purgation precedes illumination. In evangelistic terms, conviction precedes salvation. But in practice there is little time allowed for a profound experience of "conviction", especially in recent years when the crusade sermon is limited in time by the exigencies of television programming. In one relatively short sermon Graham has to lead the soul through the experience of its own sinfulness and helplessness, of its felt need, of assurance that Christ is the answer to that need, of possible doubts about that assurance, of their resolution and reaffirmation of assurance, of a decision to accept Christ, of confirmation of that decision, of final determination to implement that decision by "coming forward". This is the pattern in a typical crusade sermon, given in 45 minutes, maximum. In these circumstances it is easy to see how the experience of conviction of sin and need of Christ can sometimes not be implanted very deeply or experienced very profoundly even when a person comes to the crusade more than once.

Hulse, who, as a counsellor at first enthusiastic about the crusades, worked with the inquirers at the London crusade of 1956, says that the first seeds of disillusionment were sown then, when he talked with some who came forward: "The absence of conviction of sin was marked and disturbing". Those who came forward at the crusade meetings in New York this author attended, if they were experiencing any profound conviction of personal sin, kept it strictly to themselves. I didn't see a wet eye in the crowd, or even a damp one. Of course, this is a very difficult thing to judge. Lack of such external signs is no proof that there was no deep realization of personal sin. On the other hand, in these circumstances, there is no proof that there was, either. The predominant motive for coming forward and accepting Christ might have been simply the benefits to be derived. This brings us to our next point.

Does Graham Offer a
Simplistic Notion of Salvation?

Graham has been accused of offering a salvation that is (1) too easy, and (2) ignores the complicated social dimensions of Christianity. Reinhold Niebuhr wrote that at the Graham rallies people are offered "a new life, not through painful religious experience, but merely by signing a decision card. Thus a miracle of regeneration is promised at a painless price by an obviously sincere evangelist. It is a bargain".

This charge is inaccurate and unfair. Graham has said that coming forward and signing a decision card does not work a miracle of regeneration. We have already noted that since the very early years those who come forward are not called *converts* but *inquirers*.

There are two ideas here that have to be carefully distinguished: one, being a Christian is a "bargain", as Niebuhr puts it colloquially, and two, becoming a Christian is easy. As for the first, Scripture itself assures us that conversion is a "bargain" in the sense that what we receive is infinitely worthwhile and infinitely superior to any effort we may put forth in acquiring it. The pages of Christian hope in the New Testament are full of this thought: "The sufferings of this life are not worthy . . ." (*Rom* 8:18), "the weight of eternal glory out of all proportion . . ." (II *Cor* 4:17), "Eye hath not seen . . ." (I *Cor* 2:9).

But this does not mean that becoming a Christian, adult and mature, being really converted, is easy. Scripture and the masters of the spiritual life assure us of the contrary. Graham himself is aware of this, as we see from various statements scattered here and there throughout his sermons. It must be admitted however that the dominant impression he gives of the conversion process is one of simplicity and ease. "You can decide right now that you want to be born again". And the constant insistence on immediate decision, decision now, that we have noted, cannot but implant and emphasize an idea very close to this one, that decision should be not only immediate, but easy. All you have to do is accept Christ, receive him, give him a chance, surrender. This is the constant refrain. With this, the benefits are stressed. This is what you receive when you receive what he offers: sonship, you are an heir, you receive peace, spiritual life, the joy of Christian fellowship, new strength, physical benefits, continual divine wisdom and guidance, a true view of the world. Elsewhere he calls these benefits by different names.

Of the ten sermons given at Madison Square Garden in New York in 1969 and published as a book, analysis reveals that there is very little stress or even attention given to the sacrifices necessarily entailed in our accepting and following Christ. Of the ten sermons one was unusual for a Graham crusade sermon in that it was wholly devoted to the sacrifices involved, and was given throughout as a direct challenge to generosity and even heroism. But this is far from the usual stress. Of the other sermons, two had no reference at all to any difficulty or sacrifice. The other seven had such references varying from two lines to seventy-five lines: 10, 12, 3, 2, 5, 75, 27. Since the sermons ran on an average around 500 lines, this means about .4% to 15% of the sermon time was devoted to this theme.

Another Niebuhr criticism was that Graham's idea of sin, conversion, and Christianity ignores the social implications of the Gospel and is of little use for solving the complicated social issues of the day. Niebuhr wrote of "the almost complete irrelevance of his type of Christianity to the collective problems of our age". . . . "The irrelevance of this faith is derived from his wholly individualistic conception of sin and his perfectionist ideas of grace". Being converted in Graham's sense may solve personal problems like alcoholism and adultery, but does not begin to solve the great social and political problems of our time.

But it is not at all clear that Graham has a "wholly individualistic concept of sin". He says that tax dodging is thievery, insists on the obligation of tithing, and of giving liberally to charitable causes, insists on our obligation to help the poor not only in our country but all over the world, and condemns the church for not being the pacesetter in solving the racial problem. This was back in 1953, when he was writing on "The Social Obligations of the Christian" in his book *Peace With God*. Far from being individualistic in his morality, he insists that conversion result in a new orientation, new attitudes, also in the social sphere, and points to the changes that Christianity has made in the patterns of society in the past:

Many people have criticized the so-called "social gospel", but Jesus taught that we are to take regeneration in one hand and a cup of cold water in the other. Christians, above all others, should be concerned with social problems and social injustices. Down through the centuries the church has contributed more than any other single agency in lifting social standards to new heights. Child labor has been outlawed. Slavery has been abolished. The status of woman has been lifted to heights unparalleled in history, and many other reforms have taken place as a result of the influence of the teachings of Jesus Christ.

And a little further on:

The heritage of the labor unions comes from the church

and the mighty Wesleyan revivals of the eighteenth century. Social liberty for the working classes began when a Christian leader, Lord Shaftsbury, in the face of bitter family opposition, led a lifelong crusade for better working conditions, shorter hours, more pay, and fair treatment for the working man.

As for his perfectionist ideas of grace, it is true that Graham sometimes talks as if the converted Christian were a perfect man. Conversion produces a "radical transformation in human nature". "When we are born again, we put off the old man—we do not patch him up". Such a born-again Christian seems, on Graham's presentation, to be so radically new and different that he will not only be well nigh perfect himself but a powerful force for good, able to change the society around him. Christian, really Christian, labor leaders would lead the laboring man of America to repentance and faith in Jesus Christ. In New York City he declared: "What if a teenager who had received Christ were elected mayor or borough president and put into practice the Christian principles by which he lives daily? What a revolution!" This naive assumption, since somewhat modified, that if only Christians were running society, radical reform would quickly ensue, does not take into consideration either the immense complexity of social problems today, which are not immediately or easily solved, even by total good will of all concerned, nor the moral ambiguities and imperfections that remain even in a Christian after conversion. Niebuhr points out that Graham's perfectionist ideal of the converted Christian is a departure from "Luther's insistence that righteous men are still sinners". From the Catholic insistence too, we might add, in a different sense.

Does Graham really mean that evangelical conversion and the conquering of sin would solve all our problems? He says, typically: "We're suffering from only one disease in the world. Our basic problem is not a race problem. Our basic problem is not a poverty problem. Our basic problem is not a war problem. Our basic problem is a heart problem. We need to get the heart changed, the heart transformed. That's why Jesus said you must be born again. You must have a new nature, a new heart, that will be dominated by love". The implication is that once the sin problem is solved, everything else will be solved rather easily. This is of course an oversimplification. The "sin problem" will never be completely solved, nor should people be led to believe that it ever will; nor in fact would its solution lead automatically to the solution of other problems. For unfortunately, sin is not the only disease from which we suffer. Man, even converted man, would still be beset by ignorance, disease, and many other natural and physical limitations, which he has precisely as man, fallen man.

But in making the point that sin is the *basic* problem, the *basic* disease of man on earth, Graham is rendering a real service, and making a necessary corrective to the rational liberalism of the secular humanists and the Christian liberalism of many contemporary theologians. Conversion of heart is certainly not *sufficient* to solve the problems of society. But it certainly is *necessary*. Without it, no lasting solution is possible. This is Graham's basic position (which he unfortunately sometimes overstates), and in this I believe he is correct. There remains the problem of accounting, in Graham's scheme of things, for the place of the good, decent non-Christian humanist in a pluralistic society historically inspired by Christian ideals. But this problem is not an insurmountable one, unless it is supposed that humanist and Christian ideals are in irreconcilable conflict.

Thus, Graham, though sometimes seeming to present evangelical Christianity as a panacea for the ills of society, will be found generally, on closer examination, especially in his later sermons, to be advancing it rather as a *sine qua non* of such a remedy. On the race question for example he quotes with approval Senator Hubert Humphrey's comment on the civil rights laws, "Legislation alone can't do it. It has to come from the heart". Niebuhr was preoccupied with the explicit application of the Gospel to society, but Graham prefers to apply the Gospel to the individual, on the theory that good individuals generally mean good society, and social reform without individual reform is impossible. Niebuhr's application of the Gospel to society was a direct one, Graham's indirect. He prefers to work at the problems of society through the problems of the individual, not vice versa. He believes that the most important thing in the world is the proper relationship of the individuals to God in Christ, and refuses to be distracted from this task, even by very praiseworthy social causes. Nothing takes priority over this, and once this is assured, the possibilities of reforming society are greatly improved.

Is Graham Guilty of Uncritical Biblicism?

Niebuhr, speaking of Graham's handling of Scripture, said that "Graham's uncritical biblicism was a hazard to the acceptance of the Christian message by anyone who is in touch with any of the disciplines of culture, including biblical scholarship".

We have already seen that Graham is not an old-fashioned fundamentalist in the sense of being a strict literalist. He does not propose that heaven, for example, consists of ivory palaces. He accepts the principle that this is "merely oriental imagery" used to describe heaven. This, in reality the principle of literary form, leaves him free to adopt interpretations based on sound biblical scholarship.

But has he in fact done this? It must be admitted that generally he has not. He either ignores the results of biblical scholarship or looks on them with a wary eye. Some of his interpretations are literal, while others are fanciful. Thus we find him, as recently as 1969, stating that Methusalah was aged 969 years. Why did he live so long? Well, his name means "When he is dead it shall be sent". As long as he lived, God would not send the flood. But the day he died, the flood came. Noah took 120 years to build the ark. In the same sermon he repeats his favorite interpretation of Daniel 12:4—"many will wander this way and that"—as meaning a great increase of travel, "one of the signs of the end of the age". In another sermon in the same crusade, he comments on David's choice of five stones: "Somebody asked why he had five stones; he only needed one. Someone pointed out that Goliath had four relatives, and David had a stone for every one of them". Moreover he consistently interprets whatever Jesus says in the eschatological discourse as said about the Second Coming, whereas reputable commentators point out that Jesus is speaking, in a manner difficult to interpret, of both the Second Coming and the fall of Jerusalem.

Billy Graham is, on his own admission, not an intellectual. He is not an intellectual in the sense of being scholarly. But he is an intellectual in the sense of being interested in ideas. At one time he was seriously considering taking a leave of absence from the presidency of Northwestern Schools and reading for a doctorate at Oxford. He is an extremely intelligent man by all accounts. This makes his uncritical biblicism something of a puzzle.

One who holds the orthodox faith that Graham holds, in common with other orthodox Protestants and with Roman Catholics, need fear no efforts of modern biblical scholarship that are based on the sound principles outlined by Pius XII in his great encyclical *Divino Afflante Spiritu*: the importance of the literal sense, the need for history, archeology and other sciences to understand more perfectly ancient modes of thought and writing, the importance of recognizing the difference between various literary forms, and so on. The thoughtful person must see that, as Vatican II insisted, in order to learn what God wanted to communicate to us in Scripture, we must investigate the intention of the sacred writer, and we cannot do this except by paying attention to the literary form he is using.

It would seem that Graham, on his own principles, is not far from accepting these principles of interpretation. Let us hope that the growth which "Graham watchers" speak of may extend to this area also, that his Christian kerygma may be acceptable to a much wider circle, made up of intelligent as well as sincere people, for whom the narrow and sometimes distorted "biblical truth" occasionally presented by Graham can only dismay, and perhaps even repel.

Is Graham's Theology Too Thin?

He does not spell out in much detail the implications of his message, does not teach or explain much beyond the essential kerygma, does not open up the wider perspectives his message makes possible. A critic speaks of his as "a form of faith that must be irrelevant to any mature person who is aware of dimension of life and of spirit far beyond those comprehended in Graham's evangelism".

K. Chafin replies to this sort of criticism: "Those who object to presenting the Gospel and calling for a decision must realize that Graham's own statement of the limited nature of his goals does not include the totality of Christian life. He is an evangelist".

Graham himself proclaimed the limited nature of his goals after ten years of evangelism:

First, I recognize more clearly today than I did ten years ago the narrow limits assigned to the evangelist . . .

The Scriptures indicate that when Christ gave gifts to his church, one of the gifts was that of the evangelist (*Eph* 4:11). Philip was called an evangelist, and Paul told Timothy to do the work of an evangelist. Yet some in the church refuse—to the detriment of the church— to recognize this particular gift that has been given to some men.

The message of the evangelist is "narrow". It does not spread-eagle out into the broad ramifications of a total theology or sociology. Contrary to the opinion of some, the evangelist is not primarily a social reformer, a temperance lecturer or a moralizer. He is simply a *keryx*, a proclaimer of the good news, which in capsule form is "Christ died for our sins according to the Scriptures . . . was buried, and . . . rose again the third day, according to the Scriptures" (I *Cor* 15, 3f). This terse proclamation stretches over the broad frame of man's basic need. It declares that man is a sinner, that Christ is the only Savior, that Christ lives evermore and that the Scriptures are trustworthy. . . .

The Evangelist must have a high Christology. The 1928 Jerusalem conference of the International Missionary Council stated: "Our message is Jesus Christ". And as D.T. Niles of Ceylon has written: "No understanding of Christian evangelism is possible without an appreciation of (the) nature of the Christian proclamation. It is not an affirmation of ideals which men must test and practice. It is not an explanation of life and its problems about which men must argue and with which in some form they must agree. It is rather the announcement of an event with which men must reckon. God hath made him both Lord and Christ. There is a finality about that pronouncement. It is independent of human opinion and human choice". And Jesse Bader: "Whatever else the content of the evangel may be, at least it contains these three facts about the nature, life and mission of our Lord Jesus Christ—His incarnation, crucifixion and resurrection".

In another article, he quoted C.H. Dodd, "It was by kerygma, not by didache, that it pleased God to save men". Then he goes on:

Although Professor Dodd may have set up and overemphasized a dichotomy when he so clearly separated these aspects of Biblical truth, he did assist me to recognize a special emphasis in proclamation needed in bringing about the conversion of those who are alienated from God. The "kerygma" therefore, is a proclamation of the facts of the death and resurrection of Christ in an eschatological and existential setting which gives meaning to the facts.

Graham therefore is an evangelist. He should not then be faulted for not preaching the whole of the Christian message, for not preaching the "didache", for not spelling out all the implications of the "social gospel". A man should be judged on the basis of his own declared goals.

But on the other hand, he should not venture beyond his self-imposed and declared goals. He is an evangelist, not a political scientist, or political philosopher or expert in world affairs. Nor is he a trained moral theologian, equipped to answer the thousands of questions that are directed to him on personal, moral matters. If he does, the results are less than satisfactory. Thus in a book called *My Answer* we find the proclaimer of the kerygma proclaiming even gambling for small stakes immoral, forbidding social drinking, even a sip or two of liquor at a party attended for business reasons, enjoining the public confession of sins: "If you have sinned against your community, print your confession in the newspaper". Surely this is something beyond the scope of the essential kerygma and the need of decision for Christ. Here there is need of a demythologizing of the puritanical integuments of the Christian proclamation. Surely a man can sip a cocktail and not thus renounce the Christ who once turned about 200 gallons of water into excellent wine at a wedding party.

There are other cases like this. A man who has for some time been stealing small amounts of money from his employer, instead of being told to make restitution in some form or other, is told to confess all to the employer, so that he can thus witness to his change of heart and conversion. He is confidently assured that the employer will regard him as "one of the most dependable workers he has". This, without knowing the em-

ployer personally, or the correspondent, or therefore
the likelihood of the employee's losing his job, or any
family obligations he might have to support a wife and
children. Another man has served four years in prison
for a robbery he did not commit. But there is a robbery
he did commit, for which he was never caught, and this
bothers his conscience. He will get out of prison next
year. He is told that he owes restitution for the money
he did steal. Good. He is also told, after serving five
years in prison for a robbery he did not commit, "you
owe it to the authorities to confess the previous robbery
and ask for mercy". It is statements like these that
make it plain how dangerous it is for the evangelist to
play the moralist, especially in a syndicated newspaper
column, in a situation where questions and answers are
in writing, limited to a few lines, thus omitting relevant
circumstances that may change the nature of the case,
and read by millions of people, some of whom in their
earnest simplicity may apply the given case to themselves, erroneously, with the danger of false consciences
and no little spiritual harm.

Is Graham Tied to the "Establishment"?

Graham has avoided taking sides on certain poli-
tical-moral questions, notably the Vietnam war, and
this has caused criticism. It is said that he is too close a
friend of President Nixon, a virtual chaplain to highly
placed leaders of the government, too allied with the
powers that be, so involved with the establishment that
he seems to have lost his freedom as a preacher of the
Gospel. The alleged proof of this loss of freedom is his
failure to speak out against the Vietnam war.

What to say about this charge? First, let's break it down into its two parts: he is too closely allied with the establishment; as a result he has lost his freedom to condemn the misdeeds of the establishment.

What about his alliance with the establishment, and specifically with President Nixon? When I questioned Billy Graham about this in September 1972 in a long telephone conversation, his first answer was "cute". "I would venture to say that Cardinal Cushing was closer to President Kennedy and the Kennedy family than I am to President Nixon." Score one for Billy Graham on the Catholics!

Then getting down to serious discussion, he said that the closeness of his relationship with President Nixon was exaggerated, and that Nixon never calls him to ask advice on government policy. Alluding to his well-known visits to the White House in the time of Presidents Truman, Eisenhower, Kennedy and Johnson, and to the fact that he had read the Bible to three of these Presidents and prayed with them, he said that the relationship with President Nixon was something else, of a different kind. It is a more personal one, a family friendship. Before he had ever met Richard Nixon, he had known his mother and father, dating back to the forties, to the time when the senior Nixons had attended one of the Graham crusades in California. Then later, when Mrs. Nixon died, he took part in the funeral service.

It might be added that Graham has played a prominent part in the White House prayer breakfasts which President Nixon introduced, and that the President attended the Graham crusade in Knoxville, Tennessee, in May 1970 and spoke to the crowd, the first time a U.S. President had ever addressed a meeting of that kind. In spite of this friendship, Graham was very careful not to endorse Nixon for reelection in November 1972. He was repeatedly asked about this by the press, but always refrained from doing so. According to T.W. Wilson, one of Graham's closest advisors, he almost did, but not quite, on one occasion in Los Angeles, when persistently questioned by the gentlemen of the press. When they finally diluted the question to, who was going to get his vote in November, all he said was, "You can probably guess." This was not a public statement of support, complete with full reasons for his choice, the kind of thing we call an endorsement. But some newspapers ran stories of the Graham "endorsement" of Nixon just the same.

Graham realizes there is a difference between political issues and religious issues and tries to keep them separate. When I was questioning him about these matters he recounted a little anecdote. It seems he and Mrs. Graham were invited to the White House for dinner. The only other people present were the President and Mrs. Johnson. It was just six days before the Democratic National Convention of 1964, and the big question for the Convention was, who would be the Vice-Presidential nominee? During the dinner the President was called away from the table several times to confer by telephone with his political advisers. He had with him a list of fourteen candidates for the nomination, and finally read off the names to the Grahams. Then he asked, "What do you think, Billy?" Mrs. Graham kicked Billy under the table. Billy grinned and said, "Mr. President, Ruth just kicked me." Johnson turned to her and asked, "Mrs. Graham, what do you think?" She replied, "Mr. President, I think Billy ought to limit his advice to spiritual and moral matters, and leave po-

litical questions to other people." Johnson's comment
was, "I think that's a good answer."

But what about the second part of the charge: that
his close connection with the Nixon establishment pre-
vents him from condemning the deeds of the establishment when he should?

In our telephone conversation Graham said he was
under great pressure to speak out in condemnation of
the war, and also to join a group called Evangelicals for
McGovern. He said that he was resisting the pressure,
that he would not condemn United States involvement
in Vietnam because for him it was an extremely complicated question, a question that could not be answered
with a "sweeping statement." He said that President
Nixon wanted desperately to get out of Vietnam, was
doing all he could to do so, and would take any means
to get out, "short of surrender."

I gathered from this conversation that for Graham
the immorality of United States presence in Vietnam
was not *per se* evident, and that, lacking the clarity of
moral perception which others attributed to themselves,
he did not feel any compelling moral imperative to condemn the United States government and to call for immediate withdrawal. "They say I am not free to
speak?" he asked. "They want me to speak only *against*
the war."

And here Graham touched the nub of the question.
Those who criticized him for not speaking out against
the war were not so much demanding freedom for the
prophet-evangelist, as seeking an ally. If Graham
speaks out condemning United States involvement in
Vietnam, he is "free." He doesn't, so he is tool, bought,
kept.

Neat, but a little too neat. This position assumed

that United States involvement in Vietnam was clearly intrinsically immoral, that it was impossible to justify it on any ground, that any failure therefore to condemn it and call for immediate United States withdrawal was due to moral obtuseness, or moral cowardice, or both. This is a judgment not shared by everybody, certainly not by the people most intimately concerned, the vast majority of the 19 million people of South Vietnam, trying desperately to escape a Vietcong-North Vietnam takeover.

Lacking the preternatural perspicacity of moral vision others claimed, Graham refused to take a stand against the war. He has not always been so silent when moral issues have been involved, even though it meant risking popularity, both with establishment and nonestablishment types. His firm stand for integration, dating back before the Supreme Court decision of 1954, which in a Southerner working a great deal in the South and drawing heavy support from there, shows courage as well as sensitivity to moral values.

But the question of the freedom to preach the Gospel is broader than the Vietnam war, which is brought up as an example of his lack of freedom. The basic problem is that political issues are not often *clear-cut* moral issues. This is not saying that political issues do not involve moral issues. Most of them do, in some way or other. But it is a rare political issue that is a *per se* evident moral issue, that is, where all the evidence is on one side, where the case is open and shut, where all the justice is on one side, all the injustice on the other, so that the rightness or wrongness of the action or policy is clearly seen by all, or by a vast majority, of all right-minded, sincere seekers after the right.

II
CRITICISMS OF CRUSADE PROCEDURES

"Crusade procedures" is used in a wide sense in this section for "circumstances that attend the crusades". The criticisms fall under the following heads: (1) most of the people who come forward are already members of some church; (2) people are psychologically directed and "manipulated"; (3) the results, when analyzed carefully, are found to be relatively insignificant; (4) cooperation with liberal churches endangers the faith of those who come forward.

Does Graham Mostly Save the Saved?

One critic says: "Billy Graham and his follow-up experts have admitted that on the average 60% of all decisions made at his revivals were made by persons already church members. In some cities like Columbia, South Carolina, the figure was over 75%". He goes on to say that in Greensboro, North Carolina, "every 'convert' interviewed had previously had connections of some sort with the churches". In Toronto the figure was 75%.

According to a study made of the Louisville crusade, 77% of the inquirers were already faithful in church attendance and at least 66% were already professing Christians. Another critic, writing of the audience at the New York crusade of 1956, says: "It was the simple, staid, sure, saved of the retrogressive churches who held the field. . . . The Church did not meet the world at the stadium. The Church met itself—its most comfortable, confident self. Convinced Christian convinced convinced Christians".

But surely preaching a vital encounter with Christ that aims at vivifying a merely perfunctory Christian life is itself a good work, and deserves commendation, not carping criticism. Graham has never said that his function as evangelist excludes preaching to nominal Christians. In fact, he says the opposite, as we shall see in a moment.

As a matter of fact, the 60% figure given above pretty well agrees with the percentage in the United States who have some affiliation with a church. The criticism above noted refers primarily to the United States, and is in reality an affirmation that Graham's converts or inquirers almost exactly represent a cross-section of the religious affiliation, or lack of it, in the country as a whole. The higher proportion of church affiliation among the inquirers in the southern crusades (Louisville, Columbia, Greensboro) merely reflects the higher percentage of church affiliation in those areas. Graham realizes that his principal target is the nominal Christian. He says, "Many have not stopped to realize that nearly half of the church members of America rarely attend church. These fringe people need a definite conversion, or at least a recommitment to Christ. George Sweazey has said: 'The evangelizing of church membership is our first duty'. And Elton Trueblood: '. . . (our) task is to try to reach the present membership of churches with a message of such vitality that all experience conversion within the church, rather than a conversion to the church' ".

People Manipulated?

Turning to the problem of "manipulation", Malcolm Boyd calls the Graham team "engineers of human decision", and McLoughlin appropriates the metaphor for the title of one of his chapters, "Specialists in the Engineering of Mass Consent". Target in his *Evangelism, Inc.* makes a great deal of the authority that is exercised over the crowd at a crusade. It is

. . . made to act as one, standing or sitting or praying when told to do so. For example, Cliff Barrows will keep everybody standing for several minutes between verses of a hymn while he tells a story, or he will make the choir repeat a line or two for the crowd to hear how it *should* be sung, and so on . . . all thus being encouraged to obey instructions, to get used to the idea of obedience, to do what other people are doing *when* they are doing it, not to remain out of things, not to be different, not to be awkward, not to remain one among many, alone, unwanted and unloved, but to belong, to join, to imitate, to be part of the great movement: all constituents of the condition which Karen Horney has termed 'neurotic submissiveness'.

This condition tends to the abdication of individual responsibility for events, to dependence on others, on those in charge, on those who *know*, on Leaders, on God . . . and the more powerless to influence events such a person feels, the less of a person and more of a grain of sand in a desert of sand, the more important appear those who *are* in charge, who know what they are doing, who have confidence, who are not at all frightened of what is happening, who are controlling, giving orders, and having them obeyed.

Target also lays great stress on the role of music, which has the role of "unifying the crowd still more". The hymns lead the individual to identification with the crowd as an even more compact unit. The hymns in content are "auto-suggestive" and sentimental. They also have "another important, though slightly less obvious, function".

As Aldous Huxley has pointed out, "Prolonged and continuous shouting or singing may produce similar, but less strongly marked results (that is to the inhalation of a mixture of seven parts of oxygen and three of carbon dioxide, or to yogic breathing exercises). Unless they are highly trained, singers tend to breathe out more than they breathe in. Consequently the concentration of carbon dioxide in the alveolar air and the blood is increased and, the efficiency of the cerebral reducing valve being lowered, visionary experience becomes possible".

Boyd objects to Graham trying to "sell" Christ as though he were a product like soap. The Gospel should not be preached with psychological tricks, or presented in such a way presumably as to be overly attractive.

The English psychologist, Dr. Sargant, is invoked by Target, and a comparison is drawn of Graham's psychological "engineering" and the cases narrated by Sargant:

Briefly, William Sargant demonstrates that the "physiological mechanisms which make possible the implantation or removal of behaviour patterns in men and animals are analogous; and that when the brain breaks down under severe stress, the resultant behaviour changes, whether in man or in an animal, depend both on the individual's inherited temperament, and on the conditioned behaviour patterns which he has built up by a gradual adaptation to environment".

He goes on to demonstrate that those who "wish to disperse" what they consider to be "wrong beliefs and undesirable behaviour patterns, and afterwards implant", what they consider to be "saner beliefs and attitudes", are "more likely to achieve success if they can first induce some degree of nervous tension or stir up sufficient feelings of anger or anxiety to secure the person's undivided attention or possibly increase his suggestibility".

And he then supports his demonstration and proves its general truth with a wealth of examples drawn from the "better documented history" of such phenomena as the preaching of John Wesley, the conversion of Arthur Koestler to militant communism (and his later "equally intense reconversion"), the effects of Voodoo drumming and dancing, the initiation of West African boys, the use of music and terror for religious purposes in Tibet, spirit healing in Tripoli, the *Spiritual Exercises* of Ignatius Loyola, the Great Revival in Northern Ireland during the 1850's, the various manias of Europe during the Middle Ages, the conversion of Cornwall from a traditionally Catholic county to a predominantly Non-conformist one during the early 1800's, the various revivals brought about in Colonial America by Jonathan Edwards, and so on.

We have quoted Target and Target quoting Sargant at some length and let them speak for themselves, only to let them disprove their own case by trying to prove too much. Anyone who has taken the trouble to go through Sargant's book, *Battle For the Mind* knows that it is a book based on his studies of battle-fatigued and shell-shocked soldiers in World War II. A study, that is, of the extremes of emotional stress and the limits to which the human system can be subjected before breaking down. He narrates the different tricks Pavlov used to make his famous rats and dogs frantic, and draws not parallels but analogies between the physiologies of animals and man as to how reaction mechanisms work and how patterns of physical behavior are broken down under constantly increasing stress, and then built up again. This has implications, he says, in the brainwashing and breaking down of political prisoners and in certain primitive religious rites.

Without going into the merits, or demerits, of Sargant's book, we simply point out that the cases envisioned by Sargant have little, or nothing, to do with the Graham crusades. *Battle For the Mind* deals with breaking down and then rearranging behavior patterns in men who have been subjected to severe, sustained, systematic, and in the end physically unbearable stress. To equate, or even to compare, these cases with the people in Graham's crusades is sheer nonsense.

This is not to say there is no emotional content in a Graham crusade. We have already pointed out that there was some emotion, but restrained, muted, under control. We have dealt with Graham's own estimate of emotion in conversion and noted that for him it plays an important, but secondary, role.

There is no doubt emotional content in the songs that are sung. John Wesley didn't think it right that "the Devil have all the best tunes". And from Wesley's time to this, music has played an important part in evangelical piety, as it has indeed in Christian piety even from apostolic times. It is all a question of degree. In Graham's crusades the music occupies a quite modest part of the program. The people around me on the nights I attended could hardly be said to be engaged in "prolonged or continuous shouting or singing", thus increasing "the concentration of carbon dioxide in the alveolar air and the blood" and rendering possible "visionary experience".

Similarly, the sinister implications of being "commanded" to stand, sit, sing together at the appropriate times eluded me. I thought it rather necessary for 25,000 people to do these things together, if there were to be some semblance of order in the meeting. A com ment of the middle-aged minister, cited by Target, that "those fellows know what they're doing", I don't find threatening either. It's rather good they do. As for Boyd's scruples about "selling" Jesus Christ with modern "salesmanship", it really comes down to a question of taste, than which there is nothing more futile to dispute about. One must really visit a Graham crusade and judge for oneself whether he "sells too hard", whether he pushes too much, commands, insinuates unfairly, improperly or beyond measure. In this writer's opinion he does not.

Since the commonly accepted goal of any speaker is to persuade in some sense or other, and since Graham is not talking to blocks of wood, there has to be some degree of "psychological conditioning". But "psychological conditioning" is not one of those concepts that is either yes or no, like justification and pregnancy. It admits of degrees. The critics here cited see a high degree of psychological conditioning, and find sinister and ulterior purposes in what this writer takes to be indifferent, even commendable procedural details of the crusades. They conclude to such a degree of psychological conditioning as to render "decision" or "inquiry" *per se* suspect and unacceptable. With this conclusion the writer cannot agree. The degree of "psychological conditioning" involved in the crusades seems to me to be well within acceptable limits.

In this discussion of psychological conditioning, we must give the natural, psychological element its due and proper place. But we must never lose sight of the fact that we are dealing here with a phenomenon that is not only natural but supernatural as well. We have here the action of the living God in contact with the human soul in the activity we call grace. To attribute everything, or almost everything, in conversion to purely natural and human factors—the setting, the music, the excess of carbon dioxide in the body, the eloquence of the preacher, the air of command he possesses, or to some combination of factors like these—all this misses the mark. Likewise beside the mark are the assertions by various psychiatrists, analyzing from afar, that Billy Graham is a genius at the arts of communicating and persuading, that he has a special flair for the dramatic, or a special type of magnetism far beyond the ordinary, a unique charism (Malcolm Muggeridge called him "the John F. Kennedy of revivalists"). All this can be admitted—and in fact is largely true, I think—without explaining adequately the process of conversion in a Graham crusade. Salesmanship and psychology, no matter how artful, do not account adequately for what happens deep in the depths of the people who come forward at the crusades.

Insignificant Results?

Let's now take up the third criticism of the crusades—that their results, when analyzed carefully, are relatively insignificant.

The results of the crusades are perhaps the most debated and most controversial aspect of the Graham ministry. Opinions vary enormously. J.B. Priestley, after the crusades in England and Scotland in 1954 and 1955, said that he was of the opinion that only "a tiny minority are genuinely converted". The net results: "No great harm, no great good, mostly just another show". Another, speaking about the same crusades, says, "I believe the proportion of authentic lasting conversions is greater than from any previous campaign in Britain's history".

There are really four questions we should ask here: (1) How many come forward? (2) How many remain steadfast? (3) Are there other benefits from a crusade beside conversion or decision? (4) Could equally good results be obtained in some other way more easily?

1. *How Many Come Forward?* The usual percentage in an average crusade is 3-4%. Occasionally, but rarely, it will run much higher, as in Hawaii, and in Germany. But these figures are deceptive, because they are based on the attendance on a given night. If for example, one night 300 people come forward from a crowd of 10,000, the percentage given by the Graham organization is 3%. The next night, with the same sized crowd, another 300 come forward; another 3%. But many of those in that crowd have been in attendance the night before. In reality then the figure is somewhere between 3 and 6%. If 300 people went forward every night of 10 nights, on which the average nightly attendance was 10,000 making a total "attendance" of 100,000, and if only half of these 100,000 were "repeaters", i.e., in attendance on even two nights, that would mean 50,000 *people*, (instead of *attendance statistics*) and a percentage of 6%. From Billy Graham on down, the team urges repeated attendance, even to *every* session of the crusade. And it is clear from very many conversion stories that people attend every night or several nights. It is not at all unlikely that a total *attendance* of 100,000 might mean in reality only 50,000 *persons*. It may mean, especially in certain areas of the United States, only 35,000 *persons*. This would lower the attendance figures, but increase the percentage of those who come forward.

As for total numbers of "decisions", the Minneapolis office reports, for the nine years from 1950 to 1958, over 100,000 per year. The annual average has undoubtedly increased since then.

2. *How Many Remain Steadfast?* It is on this precise point that there is the greatest controversy. Unfriendly critics single out surveys that indicate meager results. Thus Target mentions an investigation conducted after the San Francisco crusade, which claimed 28,898 inquirers. The survey indicated, he says, an increase of only 200 in church attendance out of this number, after 94% of the inquirers had been contacted. A survey in Toronto made six months after the crusade showed an 80% "falling away" at that time. Target stresses the large proportion of young people under 18 who were counselled during the first week of the 1966 Greater London crusade, almost 73%. McLoughlin notes that 22,000 out of 55,342 decisions made in New York in 1955 were made by persons under 21. The implication of course is that young people, besides being suggestible, are inconstant. McLoughlin mentions the surveys made in England after the 1954 crusade. The London *Evening Standard*, from a very limited survey of 20 Church of England ministers on a basis of 336 decisions, found that there were 226 who were already churchgoers, and of the remaining 110 only 35, or 31%, were still attending church eight months after the crusade. Another survey, made on a larger scale by the *British Weekly*, showed that of 3,222 decisions, 51% were made by those who were already church members or churchgoers. Of the remaining number 64% were attending church regularly 10 months after the crusade.

It is clear that these two surveys differ notably, and widely differing conclusions are drawn from them among churchmen and students of religion in Great Britain. The Highet survey in Glasgow did little to make things clearer. It was a census of church attendance and membership. He took three counts, one a year before, the second a month after the Graham crusade, the third a year after, of both membership and attendance. This showed church membership for the three times at 203,430, 202,035, and 207,232, and church attendance at 56,503, 67,078, and 62,224. In other words, an increase, and then a decrease in attendance, and, strangely, a decrease, and then an increase in membership. These results are inconclusive because some churches outside of Glasgow are included, and Graham's crusade was only part of a large scale campaign in Scotland at the time to reach the unchurched.

On the other hand, one of the members of the Graham team assured this writer that 80% of the inquirers persevere. Graham himself is optimistic about the results, in a general sort of way. "The seed has sometimes fallen by the wayside and for many inquirers no lasting effects can be observed. They are not converted. For some the seed fell and sprang quickly up but could not withstand when difficulties arose, and withered. But it cannot be denied that an impressive majority reveals a clear and lasting change that can be called conversion".

A really objective study is required, with adequate sampling from a really representative cross-section, both in the United States and abroad, with clear definitions as to what is meant by "inquirer" (one who makes a first-time "decision"? one who rededicates himself? one who receives "assurance of salvation"?), "perseverance" (in church attendance? church membership? active apostolate? continuation of spiritual practices like prayer and/or Bible reading?), the length of time elapsed before a person can be said to "persevere" (one year? two years? five years?), and conducted by those who have no bias for or against mass evangelism in general or this style in particular, and who have no connection with the Graham organization. This kind of a survey has not yet been done. Until it is done, the perseverance of the "decision makers" must remain an open question.

3. *Are There Other Benefits from a Crusade besides Decisions for Christ?* Some say that it would be taking too narrow a view to limit the benefits from a crusade to those who come forward and sign a decision card, still less to the numbers of new members added to the churches. Besides the new Christians and the confirmed Christians that the crusade headquarters are informed of by the reporting system, there must be thousands of people who make decisions for Christ and who never write in, especially in these later years of television broadcasts on national and regional hook-up, and latterly on European hook-up as well (in 1970 to 35 European cities in 11 countries). These telecasts reach millions. There is no way of estimating the number of those who have been affected, even made decisions for Christ, without ever writing to the Graham headquarters. It must run into the thousands, perhaps tens of thousands.

In addition to this sort of result, there is another sort, of a completely different kind. Churches, ministers and congregations who formerly did not know of one another's existence, find themselves working and praying together in a common cause, the crusade. They get to know and respect one another. Barriers are broken down, and a kind of practical or grass-roots ecumenism is the result. The rest of the population too is informed of the crusade—with all the publicity, they can hardly miss it—and interest in religion is stimulated, questions are asked, seeds are planted. Graham says:

There are other results of the crusades that cannot be minimized. I am convinced that a crusade brings a new unity, a new vision and a new sense of dedication to the churches of the community. I am convinced that the conscience of a community can be deeply stirred when the churches in our great metropolitan areas coordinate their efforts in mass evangelistic campaigns.

Then he goes on to add a realistic note:

At the same time I must realistically face the fact that the crusades are no "cure-all" for the church or the community. Though lives are changed and some churches are revived, only a dent is usually made in a community. Someone had the audacity to argue that because the crime rate in New York City was not radically lowered as a result of our crusade there, the crusade was a failure. Only if the persons responsible for New York's crime had made an open commitment to Christ could such an argument have validity and make sense. Evangelism is not "magic" nor does it affect people who isolate themselves from it.

4. *Could Equally Good Results Be Obtained More Easily in Some Other Way?* This has been claimed. An immense amount of manpower, effort and money goes into the Graham campaigns. If the same amount of effort, manpower and money, it is said, were put into other evangelistic efforts, for example visitation evangelism undertaken by each of the churches, as good or even better results would be seen.

The claim is theoretical. No one knows if the results would be as good, because no one has tried visitation evangelism or some other type of evangelism on the Graham scale, or with that kind of organization and manpower. Nor is anyone likely to do so in the foreseeable future. As it stands, the question is unanswerable. Meanwhile Billy Graham and his organization continue to accomplish what they are accomplishing.

Is Graham Too Involved with "Liberal" Churches?

We have seen that this charge has been made by orthodox and ultra-orthodox critics. Graham has changed his policy in this matter: at first he only accepted cooperation from those who held the same orthodox and traditional creed he did; later he accepted support from the ministerial associations even though many minister members were not so orthodox, provided he himself was in no way impeded from preaching the pure Gospel message as he saw it. The difficulty with this is that the converts are turned over to the cooperating ministers afterward for instruction, Bible lessons, spiritual direction, etc.

Here Graham has a real problem. He cannot reach the large crowds he does reach if supported only by those of his own theological views. Widespread support from ministerial associations is necessary for large crowds. But this widespread support means the likelihood of channeling inquirers into some "doubtful" or "liberal" churches. This is the dilemma: either smaller crowds and hampered ministry in preaching, or larger crowds and the risk of dubious results. Graham has chosen the second horn.

There are delicate questions which might be raised here about moral obligation toward those whose faith has been born or revivified at a crusade. Practically, however, other considerations enter in and make the difficulty less pressing. The really "radical" or "liberal" ministers usually have little or nothing in fact to do with a Graham crusade, even though the ministerial association to which they belong is "on record" as supporting it. It is only the individual cooperating ministers who are given converts or decision-makers. The greater part of these actively cooperating ministers are presumably presiding over churches "where Christ is preached".

This lessens the difficulty, but it does not remove it entirely. It seems very likely that an unknown number of inquirers fall away from the faith because of these kinds of contacts. Graham seems to accept this, in view of the greater number of people he can reach with his message, precisely because of this broad cooperation.

7. Evaluation by an Individual Catholic

Up to now we have been taking as a point of departure the judgment of others, giving their opinion of Graham, then evaluating and commenting on it. Now let us make our own direct judgment on Graham, trying to make as fair and objective an evaluation of him as possible, from the point of view, be it clearly stated, of a moderately conservative Roman Catholic.

First, as to his statement of the orthodox Christian faith—the traditional doctrines like the Trinity, the divinity of Jesus Christ, his virginal birth, his atoning death for the sins of the world, his bodily resurrection, his return in glory in the Second Coming—we have nothing but agreement. We should also add to this list the inspiration and "inerrancy" of Scripture, with the qualification that Graham understands these concepts in a different way than Catholics commonly do. There are other doctrines as well: the fall of man, sin, hell, judgment, the miracles of Christ, the truth of the Gospel narratives, and so on. Graham's clear statement of the essential "faith handed on to the saints" is a gain, it seems to me, in these days of groping doubt and uncertainty. The Graham catechesis is refreshing, in contrast to some other less forthright contemporary statements.

Second, on the question of faith, which for Graham is an essential element of conversion, we also are in substantial and general agreement. The faith that Graham proposes is multifaceted. It is an assent of the mind, since it is a belief in certain statements of God's word. That to which assent is given is proposed as objective truth, so that we are not speaking of mere feeling. Graham has notably toned down the old evangelistic emphasis on "assurance of salvation", which so often became an emotional state of mind after a "religious experience". Graham insists often that the "facts" precede the "faith". The motive for the mind's assent is God's authority. But this is only one dimension of faith. Faith is also an engagement of the will and the affective side of man in a complete surrender to God, which includes not only the acceptance of revealed truths but voluntary submission to grace and trust in God's promises. This confident trust in God's promises is the old evangelistic "assurance of salvation" transmuted into something quite acceptable to a Catholic. In fact, Graham's idea of faith is in the mainstream of contemporary Catholic thought and agrees with what has been authoritatively proposed by the Church's magisterium.

Thus, the Constitution on Revelation speaks of an "obedience by which man entrusts his whole self freely to God, offering 'the full submission of intellect and will to God who reveals' ". The Holy Spirit in the act of faith gives "joy and ease to everyone in assenting to the truth and believing in it". The Council gets away from a too intellectualist account of faith and emphasizes Christian faith as not simply an assent to a list of propositions, but rather a personal engagement, an encounter, a continuing act of loyalty and self-commitment offered by man to God, or rather, answered by man to God in response to his loving invitation in revelation. As Father Latourelle in his *Theology of Revelation* puts it:

It is thus that faith is frequently described by Saint

Paul and Saint John: a total attitude of the whole man responding to God's advances, as an indivisible totality, where knowledge and love are only one in the spiritual impulse of the whole person. The faith which works through charity (*Gal* 5:6) is knowledge and commitment of the whole person: it accepts the whole truth of God and gives God the whole human heart.

This concept of faith is in thorough agreement with Graham's idea of faith as total engagement, adherence and commitment.

Third, concerning his use of the Bible, we have some reservations. Underlying the uncritical biblicism noted above is Graham's concept of how to interpret Scripture, and Scripture as the sole rule of faith. Graham's "the Bible says" simply is not enough. We have to get at "what the Bible means". It is impossible to read and understand, in an English translation, without further explanation and commentary, what was written down for people living 2,000-2,500 years ago, in vastly different cultures, with greatly different thought patterns and hence modes of expression. He who runs may not read this Book. We cannot understand "what the Bible means", and hence "what the Bible says" to us, without heeding biblical scholarship. Otherwise "the Bible says" some things that are impossible for an intelligent man of today to accept, e.g., a world 6,000 years old, made in six calendar days of 24 hours each, men over 900 years old. These are just a few of the more obvious examples; there are many, many more. Without a frank recognition and more frequent and consistent use of the principle of literary forms, which, after all, was used by Augustine, Chrysostom, Jerome and others long ago, as well as other more recent achievements of solid, orthodox, Christian scholars, and without changing the inadequate formula, "the Bible says" to "the Bible means" or "the Bible says, and means", Graham is severely limiting his effectiveness. He is limiting his effectiveness because, in his hands, the Word seems not like irruption of the living God into our narrow little world, and so above reason, which it is, but rather against reason, which it is not, and so barren instead of fruitful for men of today.

As for the rule or norm of faith, Graham, in the classic Protestant tradition, accepts the Bible as the sole rule of faith. He says, "I do not continually distinguish between the authority of God and the authority of the Bible because I am confident that he has made his will known authoritatively in the Scriptures".

The objection the Catholic offers to this is: How can God make his will known "authoritatively" in the Scriptures, if it is not clear what the Scriptures mean?

Who then will make it clear? For the Catholic, it is not himself, nor is it any individual Christian, or group of Christians. Nor is it, in the last instance, the biblical scholar, or any group of biblical scholars. In the last instance, it is the Church, assisted by the charism of the Holy Spirit, with the Church always, even to the end, who in her teaching office, interprets Scripture authentically. This is where a Catholic has to part company, regretfully, with Graham.

Fourth, a discreet use of "apologetic" in Graham's preaching would seem to be in order. True, Graham is an evangelist, and we should respect the limited goals which he has set for himself, not impose on him goals of our own choosing. His self-declared goal is to preach the *kerygma*, not give the *didache*, or teach a theology, or spell out in much detail the implications of the Gospel, social or otherwise. Still, an evangelist should defend and protect the very evangel itself, when it is either attacked or in danger of being misunderstood. Further, he has to present it in such a way that it is "presentable", that is, rendered acceptable to the men of his time, without in any way weakening or diluting it. He has to preach the Gospel to people "where they are" existentially, psychologically. And today, many people are under an uncomfortable impression that, if they become Christians in their hearts they must be heathens in their minds, that to accept the Gospel they have to give up reason, for the Gospel is against reason. It behooves an evangelist, even as evangelist, to dispel this misapprehension.

Many of Graham's hearers would welcome and be comforted, in the radical sense of that word, by this good news also, that the Bible for the last hundred years and more has withstood the most searching analysis and scrutiny of any documents in the history of our race, at the hands of hostile as well as friendly critics, and has emerged today worthy of even more respect and credence than before. Many would be struck by the classic but by no means outmoded dilemma of Christ: either a deceiver, or a madman, or what he said he was. Many would be impressed by the sign value of Christ's miracles and prophecies. These and similar considerations, familiar to a now unfortunately largely discarded apologetic, do not of course "demonstrate" the faith needed for conversion, but they prepare the way for it. They are "preambles" which show that, while faith is not strictly *motivated* by arguments from reason, it is not unreasonable to believe.

It seems that considerations like these might well be more often preached as part of the evangel, or at least along with it. Paul did this often, at Athens, for example, with his reference to the altar to the unknown god and the quotation from the poet Aratus (*Acts* 17:23, 17:28) and preaching in Lycaonia, with Barnabas, with his contrast between dead idols and the living God (*Acts* 14:15-17).

Graham uses the "preambles" to a certain extent. He preaches to the people "where they are" in the existential situation of looking for *fulfillment*. He uses the *cor inquietum* of Augustine beautifully; almost every one of his evangelistic sermons has some reference to the restless heart to whom Christ is the only one who can give peace. It is suggested that besides the restless heart for whom Christ is the tranquilizer, more account be taken of the questioning mind for whom Christ is the answer. And this should be done not by an appeal to authority, citing this famous scientist or that well-known doctor or thinker who has found Christ, but by a direct appeal to the reason of the hearers themselves. They are ready for it, being thinking as well as feeling and willing human beings. Christ and his Gospel are not maimed or mutilated by being presented to the whole man, head as well as heart.

Fifth, Graham is greatly to be commended for this preaching in such a way that he confronts his hearers with a decision, as in New Testament times, when people were confronted with the question, "What think you of Christ?" He confronts the contemporary world, the millions he can reach, with Christ, "the sign of contradiction", and demands that they reflect seriously on him. He faces them with a choice and makes them face up to the choice. And while, as noted above, we have some reservations about the precise way this is done, with insistence on a here-and-now immediate choice, the general value and force of his approach is undeniable.

The decision Graham faces his hearers with is the radical, fundamental choice *(option fondamentale)* spoken of by many modern theologians. Father Latourelle puts it this way:

A second characteristic of this encounter with the word is the seriousness of the *choice* it presents. For the word of God puts the meaning of our personal existence at stake as well as the meaning of all human existence. There is no question here of modifying our system of values in one or another detail: it is our whole person which needs a different orientation. If Christ is God, who is truth in person, then His word becomes the basis, norm, criterion for everything. Human thinking and conduct are subject to the judgment of this word. It is a question of choosing either for God or for the world, for the word of God or for the word of man. This is a question of venturing everything for everything, including life and death, including violent martyrdom or the humble and patient martyrdom that lasts a lifetime; in the strict sense of the word, this is a question of being or not being. Faith is thus a decision for God, and all one's life must revolve upon this dramatic decision which commits man down to his most intimate desires. A commitment of this nature is an uprooting of the human ego, sinking new roots in Christ (*Eph* 3:17).

The Catholic approaches this basic decision in a different way from the evangelical. For him, his orientation generally takes place at his baptism, without his even being aware of it. He is generally brought up in some kind of Christian nurture, adequate or inadequate as it may be. When he reaches adulthood he must in a conscious, mature, fully human way acknowledge, ratify, "appropriate", i.e., make his very own, this option. This usually is done in repeated acts of more or less intensity and with more or less self-awareness: in First Communion, in Confirmation, frequent Mass, Communion, confession, in prayer and spiritual reading, especially of the Scriptures, in times of missions and retreats. The emphasis is on repeated acts, the formation of habits, organic growth. Sometimes the growth results in a ratification, fully aware, free, and mature; sometimes, unfortunately, it does not. Once the basic decision is thus made and ratified, then repeated religious acts serve to rectify, sustain and vivify this basic decision already made.

Karl Rahner in his article on "Conversion" in *Sacramentum Mundi* calls attention to the importance for Catholics of the kind of decision Graham preaches:

Pastoral practice and theology, however, ought not to overlook the phenomenon of conversion as a decisive function of pastoral care of the individual. Not only because freedom in the sense of man's unique, historical self-realization intended to be final in regard to God, implies a fundamental decision *(option fondamentale)*, but also because a decision of this kind ought to be carried out as consciously and explicitly as possible, since reflection and history are constitutive of man's very essence. From this point of view, conversion is not so much or always a turning away from definite particular sins of the past, as a resolute, radical and radically conscious, personal and in each instance unique adoption of Christian life. And in this, freedom, decision as absolutely final, and grace are really experienced (cf., e.g., Gal. 3:5). Furthermore, in a society which in philosophical outlook is extremely heterogeneous and anti-Christian, Christianity in the individual, deprived of support from the milieu, cannot survive in the long run without a conversion of this kind, i.e., personal fundamental choice of faith and Christian life".

The Catholic however is very conscious, undoubtedly more than an evangelical of Graham's style, of the fact that this basic decision does not remain once-for-

all and irrevocably "decided", that it needs constant renewal, rectification, and even reratification after viola-
tion. The Catholic, who has had the concept of original
sin drilled into him, has no illusions about perfec-
tionism in "the saints". He is painfully conscious that
even the most fervent, subjectively unconditional "decisions for Christ" can and unfortunately often are nulli-
fied subsequently by the inconstant, miserably peccable
human beings who make them. He has no "assurance
of salvation" in any Wesleyan sense, even though he
has complete reliance on God's promises. He would
temper Graham's optimism about the moral capabili-
ties of the born-again Christian. He would qualify and
tend to minimize the reliance on the single act of decision, the stress on the one-time crisis conversion as a
guarantee or even a promise of a life that will be lived
forever after "in Christ". He would endorse John Bail-
lie's sage critique of "one single conversional readjust-
ment" and his quoting with approval of the saying, "the
Christian life is made up of ever new beginnings".

In justice to Graham, he himself does not make
Christian conversion consist in this one only act, "decision for Christ". He says, as noted above, that it is not
a once-for-all experience, but a step. However, he does
not say this very often, nor very loudly. It is a question
of emphasis. In truth, he seems to want it both ways,
both a once-for-all crisis-type decision that he presumes
will remain fixed (aided of course by prayer and Bible
reading), as well as a process-type conversion that is
typified by nurture and gradual growth. Graham
admits both kinds of conversion. On this point he is not
a doctrinaire evangelical.

Sixth, a Catholic finds Graham's omission of the
Church and sacraments from his preaching a defi-

ciency. While understanding perfectly well his reason for it, he cannot but feel the sense of loss. The Catholic does not regard the Church just as a help for him to live his life better before God. In an exuberant profusion, and confusion, of mixed metapors, he sees his Church as the mother who bore him, as well as the home which shelters him, the rock which is his fortress, the body of which he is a living member, the living organism into which he is implanted, an olive tree as well as a vine, and from which he draws life, a royal priesthood, a holy nation, a purchased people, a new Israel, the pilgrim people of God of which he is as fiercely proud to be part as any Israelite in any age. This sense of community, of "belonging", of what the Europeans call "solidarity", the Catholic finds missing in Graham's call to conversion.

Missing too is the vivid sense of life, nourishment, sustenance the Catholic finds in the sacraments, especially in the Eucharist and the liturgy.

As Vatican II puts it:

The liturgy is the summit toward which the activity of the Church is directed; at the same time it is the fountain from which all her power flows. For the goal of apostolic works is that all who are made sons of God by faith and baptism should come together to praise God in the midst of His Church, to take part in her sacrifice, and to eat the Lord's supper.

The liturgy in its turn inspires the faithful to become "of one heart in love" when they have tasted to their full of the paschal mysteries; it prays that "they may grasp by deed what they hold by creed". The renewal in the Eucharist of the covenant between the Lord and man draws the faithful into the compelling love of Christ and sets them afire. From the liturgy, therefore, and especially from the Eucharist, as from a fountain, grace is channeled into us; and the sanctification of men in Christ and the glorification of God, to which all other activities of the Church are directed as toward their goal, are most powerfully achieved.

Yet, in spite of these qualifications, we must salute Graham for the way he preaches Christ "in season and out of season", for the great good he is surely doing to millions around the world. Once, in speaking of the Bible he put his finger, unwittingly, I think, on the key to his own success:

Why this enduring power and universal appeal of a book so old, so often attacked? The only answer is that it speaks, as no other book can, to the heart and needs of man. Dramatically and forthrightly, the Bible answers man's fundamental questions: Where did I come from? Why am I here? What is my future beyond this life?

On a scale unprecedented in the history of evangelism, through superb organization as well as skilled use of modern mass media, with compelling eloquence, incandescent faith, and a sincerity which brings authority, Billy Graham, like the Bible, asks the fundamental questions and speaks to the heart and needs of man.

Select Bibliography

Books and Booklets by W. F. "Billy" Graham

Billy Graham Answers Your Questions. Minneapolis, 1968.

Billy Graham Talks to Teen-Agers. Grand Rapids, Mich., 1958.

Calling Youth to Christ. Grand Rapids, Mich., 1947.

The Challenge. New York, 1969.

The Chance of a Lifetime. Grand Rapids, Mich., 1953.

The Christ-Centered Home. Minneapolis, 1961.

I Saw Your Sons at War. Minneapolis, 1953.

My Answer. Garden City, N.Y., 1960.

Peace With God. Garden City, N.Y., 1953.

The Secret of Happiness. Garden City, N.Y., 1955.

The Work of an Evangelist. London, 1953.

World Aflame. Garden City, N.Y., 1965.

Sermons and Essays by W. F. "Billy" Graham

Hour of Decision Sermons. These number about 165. They are reprints by the Billy Graham Evangelistic Association of Minneapolis of radio sermons given on *The Hour of Decision.*

Decision magazine, contains a sermon or essay in each monthly issue since 1960.

Books about W. F. "Billy" Graham

There are over 70 titles. Only a few of the most important and useful are listed here:

Brabham, L., *A New Song in the South.* Grand Rapids, Mich., 1966.

Burnham, G., and Fisher, L., *Billy Graham and the New York Crusade.* Grand Rapids, Mich., 1957.

Colquhcun, F., *Harringay Story.* London, 1955.

Daniels, G., *Billy Graham, The Man Who Walks with God.* New York, 1961.

Ferm, R., *Persuaded to Live.* Old Tappan, N.J., 1958.

High, S., *Billy Graham: The Personal Story of the Man, His Message, and his Mission.* New York, 1956.

Hulse, E., *Billy Graham—The Pastor's Dilemma.* Hounslow, England, 1966.

Kilgore, J., *Billy Graham the Preacher.* New York, 1968.

McLoughlin, W., *Billy Graham, Revivalist in a Secular Age.* New York, 1960.

———, *Modern Revivalism.* New York, 1959.

Mitchell, C., *Billy Graham: The Making of a Crusader.* Philadelphia, 1966.

———, *The All-Britain Crusade of 1967.* Minneapolis, 1968.

Pollock, J., *Billy Graham (The Authorized Biography).* New York, 1966.

———, *Crusades (20 Years With Billy Graham).* Minneapolis, 1969.

Target, G., *Evangelism, Inc.,* London, 1968.

Wirt, S., *Crusade at the Golden Gate.* New York, 1959.

Articles by and about W. F. "Billy" Graham

The material is abundant, and repetitious. Only a select few of the most important articles are listed here:

Beaven, J., "The Billy Graham I Know," *The Christian Herald,* August and September, 1966 (2 parts).

Graham, W., "Conversion, a Personal Revolution," *The Ecumenical Review,* July, 1967.

———, "Does a Religious Crusade Do Any Good?" *U.S. News and World Report,* September 27, 1957.

———, "God Is Not Dead," *U.S. News and World Report,* April 25, 1966.

———, "Interview with David Frost," *Decision,* October, 1964.

———, "Man Needs New Birth," *Christianity Today,* March 29, 1968.

———, "What Ten Years Have Taught Me," *The Christian Century,* February 17, 1960.

Haden, B., "Dr. Graham, Exactly What is Evangelism?" *Presbyterian Survey,* March, 1962.

Niebuhr, R., "Billy Graham's Christianity and the World Crisis," *Christianity and Society,* Spring, 1955.

———, "Proposal to Billy Graham," *The Christian Century,* August 8, 1956.

———, "After Comment, The Deluge," *The Christian Century,* September 4, 1957.

Wiegel, G., S.J., "What to Think of Billy Graham," *America,* May 4, 1957.